piano PROFESSIONAL

Piano Technique in Practice

Murray McLachlan

Produced and distributed by

FABER *ff* MUSIC

PUBLISHING SERVICES

© 2015 by Murray McLachlan
All rights administered worldwide by Faber Music Ltd
This edition first published in 2015
Bloomsbury House 74–77 Great Russell Street London WC1B 3DA
Music setting by Mark Goddard and MusicSet 2000
Cover and text designed by Susan Clarke
Printed in England by Caligraving Ltd

ISBN10: 0-571-53935-1
EAN13: 978-0-571-53935-2

Contents

Dedicated with love and gratitude to the memory of
Ronald Stevenson (1928–2015)

Preface

In *The Foundations of Technique*, the essential aspects of a healthy and reliable approach to piano playing were discussed. The question, 'What exactly is technique?' was considered. The reply, 'Technique is about putting into practice everything that you wish to fulfil', was suggested in the first pages and used as a starting point for each chapter.

Piano Technique in Practice takes a similar approach, applying technique to essential aspects of piano playing. The book begins with self-listening skills, rhythmic awareness and sound production – basic starting points for all musicians. Technique is then explored in Part Two via a consideration of tonal colour, rhythmic creativity, phrasing and voicing. Part Three looks at the 'nuts and bolts' and mechanics of playing, such as speed, strength, stamina and control. This leads into Part Four and a broader consideration of the essential techniques that need to be cultivated in order to develop musical assimilation in daily practising, sight-reading, fingering and memorisation.

As with *The Foundations of Technique*, the information presented in this second, more detailed, book is for all levels of pianists. It is for everyone interested in piano playing. I firmly believe that self-listening, sound production, voicing, phrasing and self-discipline can be developed from day one at the piano. Indeed, in their everyday teaching, practising and playing, pianists and teachers of all levels need constantly to consider the topics of each chapter herewith – regardless of whether they are experienced concert pianists, conservatoire teachers, adult amateurs or elementary level junior players.

It is for this reason that *Piano Technique in Practice* makes room for everyone who is interested in piano playing and teaching. In this respect the approach may be rather different from that taken in other books on technique. Many chapters begin with technical exercises and ideas that can be tackled and understood by pre-grade 1 players. What is interesting is that these have proved as helpful to the most advanced pianists as they have to beginners. Equally, examples taken from some of the most challenging works are included; as it is so easy in the 21st century to listen to repertoire via the internet, inexperienced players can follow these extracts via performances on YouTube, Spotify, etc.

Of course, each chapter does quickly move beyond the playing level of elementary pianists. But there is nothing scary about that! Pianists of all levels can understand concepts and, through an awareness of future possibilities, become inspired to develop in the longer term. It seems wrong to exclude beginner pianists from opportunities for technical enlightenment from the most exciting music available, so I give no apology for saturating the text that follows with adventurous music. Still, younger players may need to engage the attention of their parents at first in order to progress through the book, while beginner students of all ages would be well advised to work at the exercises and explanations in close association with their teachers.

This book is based mainly on articles written in recent years, but its manifestation would not have been possible without the unprompted commission from Julian Haylock back in 2000 to become a regular contributor for *International Piano Quarterly*, as it was then called. Julian's enthusiastic prompting has enabled me to build an expanding parallel career in writing that I never expected! I remain indebted to the continued support of *International Piano* magazine and Rhinegold Publishing, especially through help and encouragement from editors over the years including Chloe Cutts, Claire Jackson and, currently, Owen Mortimer.

The *Piano Professional* series is an exciting collaboration between Faber and EPTA UK. *Piano Professional* is the flagship magazine of EPTA UK and it is hoped that EPTA's values of supporting and encouraging piano teachers and their students will be given a new dimension via an ever-expanding and diversely exciting series of books relating to the piano and teaching.

Murray McLachlan, July 2015

Part 1

Listening and rhythm

1 Listening creatively

Learning to play the piano takes time! The complex mechanical difficulties, which all too easily become prime concerns, mean that there is often an understandable but deadly habit among amateur and student pianists of switching off aurally as soon as a note or notes have been articulated. Acutely sensitive self-listening is certainly not helped either by the fact that the seating position at a grand piano hardly puts the player in the best possible place to hear sounds the way an audience does as they project through an auditorium. But regardless of whether a grand, upright or digital keyboard is used, self-listening skills need to be practised, nurtured and cherished from the first lessons onwards.

Not that this is unique for pianists. The ability to listen with objectivity and sensitivity to one's own playing whilst performing and practising takes years to develop on any instrument. Indeed, precision listening is perhaps the most essential skill for a performing musician to cultivate, yet it is one of the least discussed in pedagogical literature. Because the piano is a solitary instrument by nature, young pianists are especially at risk of under-developing their listening reflexes. This is a serious technical worry, as sustainable progress and artistic development depends entirely on a player's ability to listen. Musical maturity and independence from teachers will come to students only when they are able to master the art of self-listening. 'Make your ears your tutors' is a good motto to remember every time you enter the practice studio.

One of the biggest temptations to resist is the physical exhilaration – the sporty euphoria – that can sweep away any sense of aural awareness as you play. It takes strength of character to listen consistently like a proverbial policeman, or train guard on the prowl, as you practise *pianissimo* and *molto largo* in search of unwanted misreadings, bumps and accents in the middle of phrases, or untidy pedal shifts. Beware, too, of the trap people often fall into of obsessively recording everything they practise, then listening back for evaluation. One cannot substitute an 'electronic ear' for a human one in a live performance, and to do so too much whilst practising can make you aurally lazy: all musicians need consistently to work hard at the art of self-listening. You need to develop the ability to listen without bias, to 'detach' yourself from the physical challenges of playing, and to hear with almost cold objectivity in the practice room the sounds that are being produced.

Plan–Play–Review: the threefold self-listening practice routine

From day one as a beginner pianist in the practice room, much of your time should be spent as your own critic. Practice at its simplest level consists of a three-way listening process:

1 First comes your inner conception, or **Plan** – an idealised imaginary performance of the couple of notes, half-bar, whole bar, phrase or section of

music you are about to practice. Hear an ideal performance of the fragment you are about to play in your inner ear.

2 Next comes the actual physical attempt at bringing the plan to life – **Play** what you are working at. When you play this out loud, you should do everything in your power to remain as focused as possible by listening acutely to the sounds as you produce them. Beware of switching off aurally on longer notes – it is especially important to listen-on after notes have been physically articulated. Do not get distracted by the practical–mechanical difficulties of playing the piano. These can be extremely hard to relax about, but you will manage your stress levels more easily in this respect if you can temporarily disable your visual sense as you play: close your eyes to liberate your ears! Use short-term memory to avoid staring at your printed music at the moment you are playing out loud any practice passage. I have always found blind practice extremely useful for intensifying my own self-listening faculties. It also provides lots of additional benefits from the point of view of enhancing memory skills and security. Arguably the most important benefit you get from blind practice, though, comes from the heightened awareness it provides of the sounds you produce. You should find that your ears automatically become more sensitive. It is a matter of personal taste whether you prefer to do this by practising in a darkened room or covering your eyes with a scarf, or simply by shutting your eyes.

3 The third and final stage of the self-listening practice routine involves an objective self-evaluation and **Review** of what has just been played: you self-adjudicate analytically and dispassionately what you have just heard. When you know what you want to improve in your playing, you can re-start the threefold process. Keep going by repeating each stage over and over, with repetition following repetition, until you feel that you have made sufficient progress. You can then move on to practise another section of music.

Arguably, nothing is more important for self-listening than the 'plan–play–review' practice technique, and I remain eternally grateful to Frank Merrick for outlining its principles with clarity and expertise in his seminal book, *Practising the Piano* (Barrie & Jenkins, 1960).

'Live in the now'

Pianists need to avoid living in the future or the past whilst practising! As mentioned, the basic threefold method for practising at the instrument should be used for the smallest of musical units (two or three notes) as well as for half- and whole bars, phrases and larger sections. It is especially effective if you can remain calm, patient and focused on the present rather than on the future or the past. It is vital to avoid 'end-gaining', to borrow an Alexander Technique phrase. Listen in the present. Because we have so many notes to play, we are often in too much of a hurry to leave what we have just played and concentrate on what is coming next. 'Live in the now' is therefore an excellent mantra for the practising pianist. One should never feel under time pressure when practising. For pianists, this means taking special care with offbeats, the resolution of dissonances (don't put an accent after an appoggiatura!), weak parts of the beat and long and tied notes, as well as the shorter notes that immediately follow them. Quite often our thumbs cause havoc. They are heavier than the other fingers, so if they play notes that need to remain unaccented, we need to listen with particular sensitivity in order to avoid bumps. In a more general sense, there is a tendency particularly in younger and inexperienced pianists to always accent the first note of a bar or phrase. We will look at phrasing in more detail later on (see Chapters 6–8), but a consideration of the 'touch and press' technique described in *The Foundations of Technique*[1] (preparing the keys in advance by touching them before playing), combined with an awareness of self-listening skills, will immediately lead to progress and heightened aural sensitivity.

Controlled technique: 'Never play faster than you can think' (Tobias Matthay)

Whatever you are practising, it is surely essential neither to force the tone nor to play at your optimum level of velocity. By always having something in reserve you maximise your receptivity to creativity and limit risks of tension, anxiety and vulgarity. You won't go far wrong if you simply play through your scales, études or repertoire at extremely slow speeds, *molto pianissimo*. Remember the words of Tobias Matthay ('Never play faster than you can think') and Ferruccio Busoni ('I never play loudly')[2]. These are vital: they imply that there is something in reserve; that the possibility of playing faster or louder is always there. In this way, control, poise and aristocratic effortlessness become so much easier to achieve. This is what a 'controlled technique' is all about. Its cultivation enhances self-listening.

Matthay's famous advice could easily be rephrased as 'never play faster than you can *listen*'. Nervous performers often switch off mentally and aurally as they play, with motoric reflexes working under the influence of adrenalin so that the tempo may constantly get faster without the performer noticing. Though it is almost a cliché to recommend ultra-slow practice as the basic recipe for secure stability in performance, it clearly makes sense to give yourself lots of time between every single semiquaver, and to feel that you always have lots of space so that you can really listen between the notes in all your repertoire, whatever speeds you ultimately choose. Music is full of rests, punctuation marks, breaths and tiny moments of repose. They need to be listened to. It is a pianist's duty, like a great orator, to always show and project silence and spaciousness, making sure that everything is heard and in place. This involves acute self-listening with the most critical scrutiny in practice, allowing all the notes and rests that are executed time to project with authority and power.

If you are really serious about developing your listening skills, it makes sense to slow down and work at a dynamic level that is biased in favour of a softer range

---

1 Faber 2015, Chapter 3 (page 17).
2 From private conversations with the composer-pianist Ronald Stevenson (1928–2015) at his home in West Linton, 1988.

of sounds. Slow, soft practising encourages concentration and self-awareness. It has the added benefit of making you less tired. Whether or not the human ear becomes less aware of sonic subtleties after being subjected to a barrage of loud piano playing over a sustained period of time, there is no question that your brain will cope with greater awareness for much longer if you practise quietly and allow yourself a sense of spaciousness via slower speeds. Ultimately, your ears are your best teachers, and if you develop them through this technical approach to practice, they will be able to replace your piano teachers permanently!

Recording equipment and support from friends

In order to develop your own personalised – and ultimately foolproof – internal 'sound system', you need help from teachers, recordings and sympathetic listening friends and family. Use technology and your listening supporters with intelligence, pragmatism and sensitivity. It is always fascinating to compare and contrast your own perceptions with those of others! Usually pianists are much harder on themselves than their friends are. Recordings and friends should be able to confirm or deny what your ears have just told you. They are a gauge against which you can measure progress – or lack of progress – in the self-listening stakes. Of course, when you are playing with other musicians it is very interesting to find out what others think about the balance and projection of your playing. This is especially true when you are performing piano concertos in a large hall. Many inexperienced pianists find it hard to know if they are being heard or obliterated by a symphony orchestra when they are rehearsing a big Romantic piano concerto, so having someone in the auditorium to give immediate feedback can be useful. Time and experience will, however, help in this regard (the same is true for accompaniment, chamber music and piano-duet playing), and it is really important to develop your own perceptions of balance: always try to form a clear picture of what you feel the balance is like before asking for the opinions of friends in the auditorium. If you do not do this, then you will never cultivate musical independence. Beware of trusting the opinions of others too much. Often even well-intentioned friends can be biased for social reasons when they offer criticism, praise or a mixture of the two. Ultimately, you really do have to stand on your own feet as a self-listening musician. The best piano teachers all realise this and long for the day when a student is able to work independently, using their own ears as reliable, acutely aware and sensitive 'piano tutors'.

An additional benefit of recording then listening back is that it provides you with a broad perspective of your playing. It can give a bird's-eye view and so help you to see where you stand in the build-up to a concert or exam, or just in the learning process. You can gradually develop independence through using recording devices with pragmatism. Try this recording experiment: play a page of music into a recording device, but before you listen back take detailed notes of what you thought about your playing. Consider the tonal balance, phrasing, sound quality and dynamics, as well as the mechanical accuracy, quality of pedalling and stability of pulse, etc. After writing down your immediate impressions, listen back to your recording. Does the recording tally with your written critique? If not, you need to do this exercise on a regular basis. By working in this way you should find that your listening skills become much more 'streetwise' and less naive as you practise. You can gradually wean yourself off the recording device and rely exclusively on your body's own superb audio equipment. Our ears are indeed truly excellent resources, but they need to be constantly cared for and used with intelligence and sensitivity in practice sessions. Work consistently at sensitive self-listening at the piano and your ears will develop into fabulous aural policemen/train guards, providing guidance and law and order for your playing at all times!

Warming-up listening techniques

So how to begin? The subject of developing general aural skills is beyond the scope of this book, but it goes without saying that anything you can do to develop, sharpen and extend your aural awareness away from the piano will be of enormous benefit in your work at the instrument. Join a choir, find a Kodály teacher or listen with curiosity and analytical zeal to music on the radio. The possibilities for exploration are limitless! But let's consider here warming-up as a listener at the piano. The technique of listening needs to be developed and nurtured on a systematic, regularised basis as part of your basic daily practice routine. Of course, nowadays most piano teachers and advanced players are well aware of the need to warm-up physically, both away from the instrument and at the keyboard itself. Players develop their own exercise routines to cope with preparing for what can be exhausting daily sessions of work on demanding repertoire. But the disadvantage with routine warm-up solutions is that they can – if executed without imagination – make the whole process of preparing for practice feel rather dull, and this inevitably leads to poor listening. Warming-up at an advanced level should ideally be as much about fine-tuning aural issues as about ensuring that the fingers move rapidly and healthily. It is vital to consider listening and coordination skills and inspiration, finding a way of entering 'the zone' (the point at which the player is totally at one with the instrument) from the first minutes of practise. It is therefore beneficial for us to explore some of the ways in which we can maximise excitement, sensitivity and focus in the initial stages of regular practice sessions. In this way we can prioritise the most vibrant aspects of music-making and make them a crucial part of warming-up at the piano. We should feel both excited and completely at ease when we play. Visualisation and internalisation of what we hope to achieve in the playing we are about to start are vital. But at a technical level it is all down to how acutely aware we are of the sounds we produce. Our ears provide the technical means to turn our internalised musical aspirations into reality. They are our guides, so it is important to stimulate excellent listening and sensitise our mind–ear–touch coordination skills so that they are working to optimum purpose and effect. Here are some of the ways in which an ideal combination of sensory and creative sensitivity can be stimulated in order for you to be completely focused, engaged and on top form when you tackle technical problems and exercises at the keyboard.

Single notes

Try depressing the sustaining pedal and then slowly begin playing quiet, single notes repeatedly with the same finger.[3] Listen as one sound dovetails with the next, creating a seamless flow of sonority with minimum accentuation and no sense of physical ungainliness. Try this with all ten fingers in turn. Listen at first to all the reverberation from each single note before playing the next one. You will be amazed at how long reverberation can last, though obviously its extent depends on how loudly or how softly you play each note.

Double thirds

Move on to double thirds. Use a variety of different approaches – the basic notes in the example below are merely a starting point from which to explore. Experiment with different combinations of fingering and try different keys and contrasted registers on the piano. As with the single-note exercise, keep playing slowly and quietly, but try emphasising first the upper and then the lower note in each third.

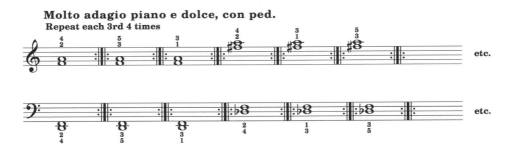

Of course, it is important to work on coordination so that when arm weight is adopted, fingers, wrists and forearms synchronise perfectly, with effortless wrist–arm alignment and no tension. It is also important to ensure that fingers really grip the keys when they are fully depressed. This should be complemented by a feeling of freedom, lightness and ease in the wrists, arms, shoulders and neck.

---

3 This is similar to the single-note scales exercise in Appendix 1, p.115, of *The Foundations of Technique* (Faber Music, 2014).

Chords

The process can then be extended to work on chords with three or more notes. Each chord should be repeated several times but with a different note in the chord receiving emphasis on each repetition. Practise by simply repeating a chord slowly, using the pedal, but balancing it differently on each repetition (i.e. bringing out the lowest note, then each of the middle notes, and finally the top note):

Hold down a large, beautiful chord, for example the opening notes of Debussy's 'La cathédrale engloutie' from *Préludes* Book 1:

Listen to the way the colours reverberate around the room, and continue listening until complete silence is achieved. You will be amazed at how long this takes. The ritual of waiting will open your ears to the care required to develop in the practising of repertoire. There are many wonderful passages to do this with, but I think that one of the most helpful practice routines for relatively experienced pianists at the start of the day is to play an excerpt from a Bach fugue several times, highlighting each voice in turn with each repeat.

The snake

Try listening to the end of each note in a phrase as it dovetails into the beginning of the next. Evidently this is the vital thing in many Russian circles, where pupils are constantly required to listen to and connect notes in as beautiful and seamless a *legato* as possible. Dina Parakhina, a former tutor at the Moscow Central Music School, refers to this as 'the snake' – a chain of connecting pitches, lovingly overlapped and gloriously reverberant. We will look at dovetailing pianism in more detail in Part 2. Meanwhile, with regard to self-listening at a more technically advanced level, let's consider the first-movement second subject of Beethoven's Op.57 'Appassionata' Sonata, bars 34–6:

Here the 'snake' is a succession of right-hand octaves. They need careful, slow practice so that they can emerge accent-free and glowing with resonance in performance. We will look at how to create beautiful sound in Chapter 4. Meanwhile, the focus in this example is on sensitive self-listening. Dovetail each octave so that one sound 'melts' into the next.

Texture

When dissecting part of a piece in the practice studio, it helps to 'zoom in' on each vertical layer in the passage in turn. This is true for even the most elementary pieces in the repertoire. Of course, choices always have to be made when it comes to performance, but it is vital that in the practice 'laboratory' the pianist observes each element in turn. This approach is also desirable with regard to highlighting different inner melodies (e.g. at an advanced level note the rising minor seconds then falling major seconds in the opening pages of Beethoven's 'Waldstein' sonata). More detailed consideration of musical layers, polyphony and texture can be found in Chapter 9.

Improvisation

Listening can be encouraged by developing the ability to improvise. This should be practised as part of the daily warm-up process at the piano. For those unfamiliar with improvisation, I strongly recommend Charles Camilleri's course in five volumes on the subject, which starts from the most modest of levels.[4] Taking ownership of the notes you are playing, as opposed to playing only music written by others, is a wonderful way of increasing confidence, as well as being tremendously enjoyable. Of course, work on scales, studies and exercises may well be beneficial in the first minutes of daily piano playing, but the priorities have to be musically and creatively led. If we can ensure that self-esteem, enthusiasm and a relaxed sense of well-being at the piano are in place, then there is every likelihood that the practice that follows a warm-up session will be infused with sensitivity and a sense of creative exploration.

Further self-listening examples

At intermediate grade 4–5 level, Grieg's 'Arietta', the first of his Op.12 *Lyric Pieces*, makes for an exquisite warm-up at the start of a practice session.

4 published by Lengnick.

Simplicity, beauty of sound, a wonderful melody and tactile pleasure are all on offer here in a piece that never fails to inspire the player towards *cantabile*, sensitive voicing, careful pedalling and awareness of flexibility in rhythm. All of these develop through sensitive self-listening skills. The piece may be only 23 bars long, but with different voicing, rhythmic variations, changes of *rubato* and subtle dynamic shifts, it will never seem dull. The same is most certainly true of the celebrated opening of Beethoven's Piano Concerto No.4, Op.58.[5]

Chopin's Prelude in C minor, Op.28 No.20, provides a wonderful means for developing self-listening skills:

This is a proverbial 'cathedral in sound', well within the technical capabilities of pianists from Grade 6 level onwards. Use it as a magnificent aural warm-up exercise by celebrating the length of every chord. It never ceases to amaze me how strong and reverberant each six-note chord can become. It is wonderful to play and re-play this piece using each of its different voices as leaders in turn.

From more advanced repertoire, the opening of Beethoven's Piano Sonata No.15 in D major, Op.28 ('Pastorale') requires acute listening skills:

---

5 See *The Foundations of Technique* (Faber Music, 2014). Professional pianists have been known to agonise obsessively over how to voice and phrase this magical musical statement. It is wonderful to experiment by emphasising each of the notes in turn on the opening chord. I recommend putting the sustaining pedal down before depressing the keys, so that the hammers are raised and minimum percussive attack is experienced as the chord sounds. Practice can then proceed with the quavers, with special emphasis taken in turn on each of the four voices in the texture. Make the phrase sound totally different as you emphasise first the soprano voice then the alto, tenor and bass in four repetitions of this glorious phrase.

Special care is required over the 'vertical hierarchy' of four voices, and sensitive aural awareness is needed for the pedal to be handled convincingly, connecting not only the tonic-pedal bass notes but also the *legato* right-hand triads. But perhaps the most challenging aspect of this passage is the phrasing in the right hand. It is only by carefully matching the decay and attack of triads and notes in the melodic line that accent-free *cantabile* and poetry will emerge.

Let's move on to a towering 19th-century masterpiece. The iconoclastic and mesmerising arpeggios at the beginning of Chopin's *Polonaise-Fantaisie*, Op.61, require exceptional control.

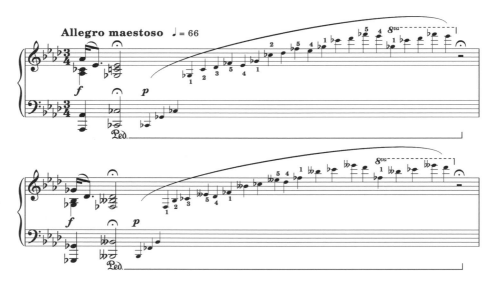

Pianists can spend a lifetime agonising over how to articulate this passage, as arpeggiated lines need to dovetail and glide effortlessly. Think of the Russian 'snake' as a starting point for practice here. In order to 'melt' each note into the next, the performer has to hide all hints of percussion from their playing, so that the end result appears executed by an instrument similar to a harp rather than one that uses hammers. And of course, everyone agonises over both the dotted rhythms and the change of colour in the first two beats of this piece. One has to listen, adjust and listen again many times for a convincing interpretation to emerge.

At the very summit of pianistic listening challenges comes late Schubert. The slow movement of his B flat Sonata, D.960, is a multi-layered listening challenge which requires precision of touch and strict rhythmic control with the left-hand figurations.

The balance between pedal resonance and due reverence to the carefully notated rests also needs to be carefully gauged, and of course it is essential to strive for a truly sustained right-hand melodic duet in thirds. It is only through patience and perseverance that success will be achieved in unfolding a convincingly lyrical – and indeed monumentally expansive – right-hand line, as the slow tempo and quick decay of the many long melody notes in this movement can easily lead to accentuation and unwanted phrase breaks.

Finally, a very famous example from the symphonic literature. Bars 1–9 in the first movement of Rachmaninov's Second Piano Concerto, Op.18, are a fabulous test for the bass register of an instrument and a glorious challenge for players in search of a dramatic, inevitable and charismatic *crescendo* from the softest of chords through to the most thrilling of *fortissimos*.

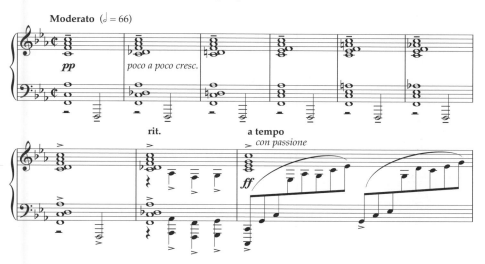

It is certainly both beneficial and interesting to prioritise different levels in the texture in turn as you repeat this iconic phrase in practice. In particular, it is interesting to give more weight and depth of tone to the thumb notes in the right hand rather than to the highest notes. It is also exciting to try to play the whole phrase in one continuous pedal, creating a wash of sound yet always ensuring that clarity and definition is achieved through careful dynamics and balancing on each chord.

2 Rhythm

In the beginning there was rhythm! Rhythm should always be considered the most important technical concern for all practising musicians. Without its clarifying logic, control and guidance, the sounds we produce are essentially rendered meaningless. Because pianists have fewer opportunities to perform with other musicians than orchestral players, rhythmic liberties and indiscretions can become entrenched in their musical make-ups. Of course, it is extremely difficult for all unaccompanied solo instrumentalists to play with an inward sense of rhythmic discipline, control and vitality. Solitary performers have to manage rhythm on their own in practice and performance, without the luxury of collaborating with an experienced accompanist or conductor, so the responsibility of sustaining a convincing pulse is left entirely to them. But pianists are at even more of a disadvantage than other solo instrumentalists because they tend to have far more notes to process and deal with – on a harmonic, contrapuntal and melodic basis. The sheer quantity of pitches on the printed page can make pianists overlook the essential requirement for rhythmic control and comprehensibility found in all the music we play. This is a basic issue and, unfortunately, an all-too-common concern for non-professional players and students of all ages and abilities.

Bad rhythm leads to confusion and anarchy on a much grander scale than the odd – or more than odd – misdirected pitch could ever achieve. Unstable and inconsistent rhythms can do more than anything else to damage security, quality and intelligibility in an interpretation. On the other hand, good rhythmic control provides interpretations with an immediately convincing structural framework. Rhythmic control acts as an essential harness for melody and harmony, giving them comprehensibility.

Rhythm should be a priority for pianists, not only in repertoire but also in all technical work, including exercises (Hanon, Beringer, Cortot, Brahms, etc.), études, scales, broken chords and arpeggios. If you focus on excellent rhythmic control at all times in your practice, you will achieve much more technical security across the board. With heightened rhythmic discipline, your whole technique will feel stronger. You will have more time to deal with awkward jumps, nasty position changes and challenging 'corners' in your repertoire. Your music-making will feel more organised and less hurried, and as a result you will become a far more confident player.

Towards rhythmic control

Sadly, rhythmic control tends to be sidelined in many technical treatises and collections of exercises. It is almost as though rhythm is not considered a technical concern in its own right. The main purpose of this chapter is to change this perception. Rhythmic control is as 'technical' an issue as clarity of articulation, building up speed, or developing a beautiful sound. Without rhythmic technique and facility, it is very difficult to do anything productive at the piano, and it is crucial that rhythmic skill is built up from the very first piano lessons.[6] A full consideration of how to develop an 'inner pulse' follows, and it involves extensive use in practice time of a famous device.

Using the metronome

In *The Foundations of Technique* we touched on the use of the metronome in a sporty sense, using it like a treadmill at the gym, with students either building up their repertoire to appropriate tempos or else targeting exciting speeds as they sweat and toil towards playing scales at crotchet = 160 (with four notes to each beat). Traditionally, with more advanced players the metronome tends to become a less essential tool, though its use for professional musicians is of course invaluable when tempos need to be checked (and this can include sessions in the recording studio, when pressure and stress can lead to significant changes in speeds between takes). The metronome's significance as a means of harnessing technical development at the piano has, however, been shockingly overlooked at all levels of piano playing. Recent conversations with the pianist Graham Caskie have reminded me of the significance of using the metronome as a clarifying agent in all kinds of technical exercises. Since its invention in the first half of the nineteenth century, it has remained an important tool for most teachers and students; a surefire means of ensuring rhythmic discipline when students meander or rush through their repertoire. Because the metronome gives rhythmic order, it demands complete discipline and control, the two things that are most important in technical exercises.

Coordinating exercises with the metronome

The metronome can help us to develop and refine our technical–rhythmic coordination. When you set the machine at a fixed number of beats and begin playing through your Hanon, Cortot or Tankard exercises, there is no room for hesitation, uncertainty or confusion. This should be obvious, but how many students do you know who regularly and consistently practise exercises with the metronome? The metronome immediately encourages you to focus on and listen to the actual space between the notes you play. It almost goes without saying that it is these silences, as much as the notes themselves, that determine the conviction and success of our performances. This is enshrined in an often-quoted remark by the great Austrian pianist Artur Schnabel: 'The notes I handle no better than many pianists. But the pauses between the notes – ah, that is where the art resides.'

---

6 In fact, many would argue that rhythmic coordination as a separate skill needs to be set up and established via Dalcroze exercises and lessons long before piano lessons even begin. Though beyond the scope of this book, readers are strongly encouraged to explore the enduring legacy of Émile Jaques-Dalcroze (1865–1950) via the society www.dalcroze.org.uk.

Preliminary exercises for rhythmic coordination

Let's move on to some concrete exercises that use the metronome and emphasise rhythmic stability in tandem with technical facility. Here are two basic preliminary percussive exercises that everyone can attempt, involving tapping in one hand and playing in the other. Set the metronome at crotchet = 80 and swap tapping and playing between your hands. For variety, you can gradually increase the metronome speed as you gain in confidence and facility.[7]

Exercise 1

Repeat with LH playing notes an octave higher whilst RH taps the rhythms

Exercise 2

Repeat with RH playing notes an octave higher whilst LH taps the rhythms

7 Further rhythmic practice similar to these exercises can be found in Paul Hindemith, *Elementary Training for Musicians* (Schott, 1946) and Paul Harris' series of books at Grades 1–8, *Improve your Sight-Reading!* (Faber Music, 2008).

We can now move on to some early, virtuosic Beethoven. Bars 16–22 of the Sonata in D major, Op.10 No.3, require equality and coordination between the hands so that evenness and rhythmic precision can emerge intact.

Forget about work at the piano for our current mission and start tapping out the rhythms on a table top with your metronome set again at crotchet = 80. Then gently pat the table with each hand in alternation, as though beating a side drum. This exercise can be used by players at every level. Start with one pat for each metronome tick. Listen for equality between the hands, and then move on to two and then four pats per tick. Place a mirror in front of you and try to keep your left and right sides equidistant and similar in approach. Remember the principles of alignment between wrists and arms outlined in Chapter 2 of *The Foundations of Technique*. Work with relaxation, economy and ease, feeling comfort and rhythmic vibrancy as you gradually inch your way up the metronome.

Telescopic rhythmic technical work, or 'musical binoculars'

In five-finger exercises, scales, arpeggios, broken chords, double-note and octave scales, it is invaluable to use the metronome as a nature lover would use a pair of binoculars. Begin by setting the metronome at the fastest possible speed, for example crotchet = 200, and then play each note of the scale or exercise simultaneously with each tick of the metronome. This is close-focus work and is important for precision and coordination from the earliest stages of piano playing.

1 Here is a typical five-finger exercise that could benefit from this type of practice:

More advanced players could experiment with the use of arm weight on each note, taking a separate movement of the arm for each quaver in turn.

2 Next, set the metronome at 100 but continue to play the exercise at the same speed. We are taking a step back and adjusting our 'musical binoculars', and the move to two notes per metronome beat makes it easier to practise playing with two notes to each arm movement rather than one. This will be helpful in building up control in two-note slur passages at all levels. It certainly is essential to master this approach before tackling the beginning of the first movement of Beethoven's Sonata in D minor, Op.31 No.2 ('Tempest'):

Once the two-note slur exercise is mastered at crotchet = 100, it is beneficial to try it at even faster speeds, always keeping the same two-note slur pattern intact.

3 The third stage is then to set the metronome at 50 bpm and to take four notes at a time in each arm movement to each metronome beat:

♩ = 50, 4 notes to one arm movement

A convincing realisation of this will see subtle but noticeable wave-like movements of your arms and wrists as you play.

4   Because not many – if any – metronomes offer a speed as low as 25 bpm, I recommend that you next tackle eight notes per beat/arm movement at crotchet = 50:

♩ = 50, 8 notes to one arm movement

This approach is especially helpful in building up a rapid scale technique, and it feels as though you are surveying the exercise or scale you are performing from a panoramic view.

Clearly, this method of working with the metronome can be extended effectively to repertoire with great effect, not only in fast, virtuoso passages but also in extremely slow movements, where it can be helpful to use the metronome to mark semiquavers, then quavers and finally crotchets as you practise.

Other rhythmic exercises with the metronome

The metronome is also extremely useful when you are working at single- and double-note trills, tremolandos and repeated notes. This is because these technical challenges demand complete awareness of the number of notes executed per beat. Here are some rhythmic trill exercises that can develop coordination and an awareness of the number of notes you are playing in trills.

This example is based on an exercise provided in Busoni's edition of the C minor Prelude from Book 1 of 'the 48' by J.S. Bach:

Try practising all trill passages in triplets. The use of the metronome in this example, and in many others of a similar nature, will instil an immediate sense of discipline and order into your technical work, encouraging excellent synchronisation between the hands. This trill exercise can be practised with the metronome set at crotchet = 84. Use small, firm but relaxed arm movements for each note, and then gradually increase the speed on the metronome until you can play the exercise effortlessly at crotchet = 160. As the tempo increases, it is easier to focus on one arm movement for six notes at a time, though I find that at optimum speed I am thinking of twelve notes in one 'wave' or arm movement as I play. As in the five-finger scale exercises above, it is a case of refocusing our musical lenses and taking a broader approach as the notes spin forth with increased velocity.

The metronome is also useful when working on awkward finger shifts, tone control and leaps, and when dealing with polyphonic challenges such as those to be examined in Chapter 9. In short, there is hardly any technical work for which it is not useful. Repetition becomes more manageable and less frustrating when a regular pulse is set up and sustained by the metronome during daily practice. It is also worthwhile returning to work with the metronome on the examples shown in Appendix 2 of *The Foundations of Technique* ('Examples of polyrhythm scales'), as well as on the chapters in that book on scales, arpeggios and broken chords. These basic patterns, including all three broken-chord variants and the 'Russian' or 'formula' scale sequences, are excellent for developing rhythmic security alongside technical demands.

There is a direct parallel between a swimmer's armbands and a pianist's metronome: both are extremely useful but ultimately need to be discarded. We will consider independence from the metronome at the beginning of the next chapter.

3 Rhythmic vibrancy

Independence from the metronome

Independence from the metronome means developing a strong internal awareness of rhythm: an 'internalised metronome' for your inner ear that is more vibrantly charged and receptive to characterisation than a mere machine could ever hope to be. This inner awareness of pulse and rhythm is best developed through focus, and awareness of breathing and movement.

Breathing

Before going any further with musical issues, remember that professional non-musicians can be enlisted to help directly with awareness and control of breathing. Whom and what is chosen for this task is entirely up to you! It could be that a Pilates class is the best way forward, though others may prefer to explore yoga, a personal trainer at the local fitness centre, or simply some exercises or the advice of an osteopath. Your local GP should certainly be able to provide advice on general health, and Alexander Technique lessons on a one-to-one basis can be illuminating and extremely beneficial.

Of course, breathing in music-making is of paramount importance for singers and wind players on both a musical and a technical level. In order to avoid ungainly bumps and interruptions to phrasing in mid flow, they need to develop highly sophisticated and skilful breath control and facility. Convincing breath control for wind players and singers fuses technical ease with musical sensitivity. Things are rather different for pianists, though breathing can paradoxically become more of an issue – precisely because you don't use your lungs to create sounds from the piano. The lack of a physical need to inhale and exhale can make it harder for pianists to project an interpretive sense of spaciousness, musical clarity and characterful phrasing. This is a serious concern, as music needs to breathe. Pianists, like all performers, need time to pontificate through skilful breath control on stage, making the most of every musical punctuation mark and enjoying what Artur Schnabel called 'the pauses between the notes'.

It is tempting for pianists to hold their breath throughout difficult technical passages, thereby making the passages in question even harder to play! We will look at breathing in relation to phrasing in Chapter 6. Here it is enough to realise that poor breathing induces rhythmic instability, which in turn leads to technical insecurity. Clearly, confident, natural and relaxed breathing is of paramount importance for developing a reliable technique that can withstand the pressures associated with public performances. In this connection I always remember the pre-concert advice of my former teacher David Hartigan:[8] 'Don't

---

8 David Hartigan (1946–96) Pianist, teacher and Assistant Head of Keyboard at Chetham's School of Music.

forget to breathe!' This was always his last catchphrase in the seconds before a performance was scheduled to begin. And, indeed, there is no better way to induce controlled rhythmic security than by consciously focusing on inhaling and exhaling. Breathing is unquestionably one of the most natural of all human impulses. When we breathe erratically, with agitation and effort, the chances are that we will behave erratically. When people are angry they are often breathless but unaware of their abnormal breathing patterns. In terms of piano playing, this translates as playing with an erratic pulse, usually with lots of speeding up, in performance. Passages will rush forward with no sense of control and pace.

A basic rule of thumb to remember for all music is to breathe during silences. Beethoven's Piano Sonata No.5 in C minor, Op.10 No.1 (second movement, bars 17–21), provides opportunities to take breaths in the rests:

Whilst it is not physically necessary to take in air in every rest, it is interesting to do so in that it certainly stabilises the rhythm and makes the music technically more convincing as a result. It is also interesting to try this without breathing through the rests, and to see what effect holding your breath has on the pulse and shape of the music at this pivotal structural moment in the piece.

When we are able to control our breathing, we are more likely to be able to control our nerves. We are more likely to remain calm, take pleasure in performance and overcome technical difficulties. No matter how easy or difficult a piece is, it can be enormously beneficial to mark down on the score in pencil the moments when you can exhale. If the music falls naturally into eight-bar periods, it is clearly essential to breathe in moments that correspond to commas, semicolons and full stops in poetic prose.

When you have good 'inner rhythm' you find a way to make all the music you perform breathe. Breathing provides you with more space and time to cope with awkward technical demands. Clearly, it is the performer's ability to breathe and mould the music's shape from within that gives rhythmic conviction to an interpretation. As mentioned already, nervous performers often switch off mentally and aurally as they play, and may be completely unaware that the tempo is constantly getting faster. It can be extremely inspiring to study in detail the playing of great pianists from the past who had the ability to sustain tempos and expand with aristocratic poise and nobility regardless of the technical demands that they faced. As great examples of control in this sense I would cite in particular many of the recordings by Claudio Arrau (a pianist who evidently almost never pressed forwards in performance) and Jorge Bolet. Both artists had the rare ability to expand and broaden passagework, creating magisterial vistas in sound that often made the music they interpreted seem even more monumental and epic (think of Arrau's approach to Brahms' D minor Concerto, or Bolet's handling of 'Vallée d'Obermann' by Liszt).

Physical movement

Performers need to be able to do much more than play the notes of a piece. They need to be able to dance, sing and breathe every phrase with total conviction and a complete lack of inhibition. Rhythmic energy is a means of achieving this. Unfortunately, the sedentary life of a pianist can induce a feeling of lethargy that is anathema to rhythmic buoyancy and discipline. Ultimately, a lack of rhythmic control in performance is due to a lack of connection with the basic pulse of the music. Security and control come from an organic connection to the music. In order to counterbalance the hours spent sitting at the keyboard, it makes sense to be physically active and enjoy dancing, moving in time to music and conducting. The relationship between piano playing and dance is a voluminous subject, and whilst I would never say it was vital for all would-be interpreters of Chopin's mazurkas to learn the steps of the Polish dance, it would certainly do no harm to do so – provided it is remembered that Chopin was not writing background dance music in his magnificent masterpieces for solo piano! How easy should it be for dancers to move to a waltz or polonaise (or even a Baroque courante) when a performer plays such a dance in recital at the Royal Festival Hall? It could be argued that a Bach or a Chopin used the dance form as a starting point for imaginative stimulus, and that it is too prosaic to simply play their masterpieces as though accompanying a class of dancers. Equally, it would be totally wrong to adopt rhythmic accentuations and tempos that completely negate the spirit of the dance on which a particular piece is based.

Anyone can experience the pleasure and thrill of waving their arms around in time to a recording at home. To do so is not to be eccentric or vain – it can be a vibrant education in itself. When you 'conduct' a recording of Johann Strauss waltzes, for example, try to feel the pulse, the lifeblood of the music, in your torso. 'Dance internally'. Feel your abdomen bouncing in time to the pulse. Try this with lots of contrasted music. Polkas, waltzes, scherzos and marches make good starting points, but eventually you should be able to really feel the rhythmic vibrancy in the whole repertoire, including slow adagios, outer movements of symphonies and entire sonatas. Once you find it easy to bounce in time to music as you listen, you can try to refine and concentrate your physical movements so that they are not readily noticeable by others. Feel a strong internal pulse but do not ostentatiously display it! By doing this, you are cultivating a strong internalised awareness of rhythm.

You can then transfer this approach to your own playing. Try playing the following examples with lots of physical movement – you can try bouncing up and down on the piano stool on each beat in the first extract, or try moving your entire torso round in slow, clockwise circular movements in the Erik Satie *Gnossiennes*. Experiment, too, with the telescopic rhythmic techniques outlined in Chapter 2 in any Classical or Baroque minuet: firstly, move your abdomen on every crotchet beat, and then try repeating the piece with stomach moves only on first beats. On the third repetition you can try moving from side to side every second bar. Finally, you can try moving your torso in a large, slow, clockwise circular movement that takes a full four bars to complete a single revolution!

Over the years, exercises such as these have proved consistently successful with numerous students of varying ages and abilities. They help inexperienced players towards greater rhythmic awareness and control. It is important to feel rhythm internally, and these exaggerated exercises are there to encourage a more open and direct connection with music's pulse – its life force. If you do not indulge in physical gesticulations in everyday life, then rhythmic vibrancy at the piano could prove challenging. You have to truly love rhythm to be able to express it in your playing with conviction. Fortunately, love of rhythm can be stimulated and encouraged through constant nurturing, both at and away from the keyboard.

Sustaining the pulse

When you are truly inside the pulse of the music you are playing, you feel at one with the character and style. All music breathes, and when you have good inner rhythm there is more space and time in which to cope with awkward technical demands. Sustaining the pulse does not necessarily mean rigid adherence to one metronome marking. Many great concert artists in their recordings fail to sustain a consistent metronome speed for more than a few bars (sometimes for even less in slow movements). But this 'failure' is in fact a success: refusal to be corseted to a metronome means that it is possible to enjoy the space between the notes. Sensitivity to this is what inner rhythm is all about. Do try as an experiment setting the metronome going as you listen to many of the great recorded performances of the Viennese classics (I am thinking of masters such as Brendel, Serkin and Arrau here in particular), and notice how they tend to fail in sustaining any one tempo for long. Clearly, it is the ability to breathe and mould the music's shape from within that gives the external appearance of rhythmic uniformity. Superficial and obsessive metronomic accentuation in performance inevitably results in interpretations that sound machine-like and dull.

In music inspired by machines and motoric drive, rhythm would seem a more straight-forward issue: is it simply a case therefore of setting the metronome at a given tempo and proceeding to play with no deviation of speed until the final note is struck? In fact, it can be extremely difficult to block out human weaknesses when tackling motoric repertoire such as toccatas by Prokofiev, Debussy or whoever. All too often the music begins to lose its requisite space, control and technical poise, which means that the structure will be unconvincing. I do not advocate an icy-cold unemotional rendering of any music: the answer here is definitely not to become detached from one's primeval instincts. Certainly it is much more fulfilling and helpful to engage in dancing and conducting to improve inner rhythm than just keeping together with the metronome.

In considering rhythmic vibrancy, it should always be remembered that subtleties are impossible to notate accurately, and that consequently it is completely wrong to become a servant to the text when dealing with dotted rhythms, not only in the Baroque period but also in the polonaise rhythms of Chopin, and even in the famous dotted-quaver motif of the 'Moonlight' sonata, Op.27 No.2. 'Giving and taking' in terms of rhythms on a small scale, as well as on the larger scale of an eight- or sixteen-bar phrase structure, will always have to come from an inner connection with the musical motivation of the piece in question rather than from written instruction. Indeed, it is wonderful that such an important issue as rhythmic freedom is impossible to notate exactly, because the lack of precise instruction on the published text means that there are many, many possibilities of execution. Ultimately, it is the performer's ability to convince that will determine how successful a particular rhythmic liberty is, and such success comes from a profound love of and connection with the music itself. Here are some examples:

1 The D major fugue subject from Book 1 of Bach's *The Well-Tempered Clavier* gains its entire personality and character from the way in which performers choose to tackle the dotted-quaver rhythms in the opening subject.

There is no right or wrong over whether or not the player chooses to double- or single-dot these notes, though of course stylistic consistency is extremely important. But it is vital that the numerous presentations of this strong rhythm are presented with watertight strength and clarity throughout, whatever decisions are taken. (Contrast here, for example, the playing of Tatiana Nikolayeva on Olympia with single dots as opposed to Bernard Roberts on Nimbus, complete with ornamental flourishes as well as double dots.)

2 In the slow movement of Beethoven's Sonata in E flat, Op.7, the rests are as vital to the character and musical intelligibility as the notes themselves, so it is essential that they are extremely well sustained and held throughout:

There can be no room for 'clipping' silences here, and the difference between rhapsodic waywardness and structural cohesiveness in contexts like this one can be very little indeed. There is even a case for consciously lengthening some of the rests in this movement. Certainly a sense of expansive elongation can add gravitas and power to many of the silences.

3 On the subject of rhapsodies, Liszt's Hungarian Rhapsody No.2 in C sharp minor (bars 9–18) demonstrates that it is totally wrong to be literal with the printed page in terms of rhythm when dance or folk elements are implied:

The possibilities for bending and enjoying rhythmic flexibility here are enormous, and authority will always arise if the player can feel conviction and inevitability as he or she plays. To reproduce the ideas of a teacher or recording here cannot lead to success unless the performer is able to dance internally to the *rubatos* they have created.

Rhythmic vibrancy and mechanical challenges: mind the gap!

Chapter 13 of *The Foundations of Technique* showed how the observation of articulation markings at the opening of Beethoven's Sonata in C, Op.2 No.3, could solve technical difficulties. In effect, the performer needs to add a gap between Beethoven's slur and *staccato* markings. Gaps between musical motifs and figurations are all part and parcel of rhythmic awareness, so it makes sense to close this chapter by exploring this aspect of rhythmic vibrancy in a little more detail.

Being aware of all points of repose, silences, and pauses for consideration and space in music is essential. We have already seen this in Chapter 2, with regard to the metronome in technical work. As pianists with so many notes to play, we can all too readily fall into the trap of forgetting that it is the rests and silences that often make the interpretation of a piece really convincing. And in down-to-earth, technical terms alone, it is this awareness of musical space – the 'gaps' between the notes – that can mean the difference between reliability and insecurity. Let's look at some of the ways in which 'minding the gap' can make a huge difference.

Firstly, it is important to remember to finish what you are doing before moving on to say something else! Too often, technical problems occur because players are thinking of the next challenge too early. Lack of clarity and control often comes at the end of a musical sentence or period rather than at the beginning. Reduce problematic passages to the smallest musical units you can. Isolate challenges and celebrate the musical space between each challenge. Being able to 'live in the present' and stop worrying about what is about to happen next is the solution to numerous technical issues. Take time when practising to radically lengthen the space between phrase markings and during rests. Before the gaps, you can experiment by slowing down and getting louder. If you work on small passages, one at a time, with repetition, *ritardando* and a consistent *crescendo* in place on each re-playing, there is much less likelihood of panic when you come to perform these passages in public. Clarity and control in articulation comes from being aware of what you are doing at all times. Exaggeration by augmentation of musical space will help with this as it helps you to focus on smaller musical units. Let's plunge straight away into advanced repertoire for examples. The exposition in the first movement of Beethoven's celebrated 'Appassionata' Sonata in F minor, Op.57, is notable in this respect in bars 52–4:

The large physical jump to the Neapolitan harmony, *fortissimo*, at the beginning of the second bar above is often untidily played. Even when the notes are executed cleanly, players too often fail to recreate the requisite dramatic power and intensity here – because they are afraid of splitting notes. By simply lengthening the space between bars 52 and 53, much more excitement, confidence and accuracy will immediately fall into place. As recommended above, it is good to try expanding on 'gaps' in practice sessions, and this is an excellent example of this. Enjoy lots of time and really make a big dramatic impact when Beethoven asks for *fortissimo*!

Next comes an excerpt (bars 22–4) from Liszt's second concert étude, 'Gnomenreigen':

Un poco più animato

This is of course a ferociously hard étude, but one that can be mastered more easily if 'mind the gap' mentality is remembered in practice. Putting space in the practice studio in between each technical 'nasty' a piece like this presents makes life so much easier. It makes it possible for you focus calmly and methodically on technical challenges – separately. In this excerpt, the final six semiquavers of bar 23 are often fudged and realised without the razor-sharp clarity they demand. I recommend fingering these notes with 2-1-2-3-1-2 whilst adopting a big *crescendo*, then dropping to a *subito piano* at the start of bar 24. The gap between bars 23 and 24 is necessary for the music to really be clear to the listener. It also provides the performer with a much welcome pit-stop break that makes life so much easier.

Part 2

Sound

4 Tone production

Many pianists are firmly convinced that they can put a vast amount of expression into the striking of a single note of the piano: some claim to be able to draw the whole gamut of emotion out of a single key. In reply, the untemperamental scientist points out that, in striking a single note, the pianist has only one variable at his disposal – the force with which he strikes the key; this determines the velocity with which the hammer hits the wires, and once this is settled, all the rest follows automatically... It seems clear that, so long as he confines himself to striking single notes, the greatest virtuoso has no greater range of effects at his disposal than the child strumming at his five-finger exercises. To put this last matter beyond doubt, three American Scientists, Hart, Fuller and Lusby, of the University of Pennsylvania, have recently made records of the sound curves of single notes played by well-known virtuosi, and also of the same note played by letting a weight fall on the keys ... No visible difference can be detected.
(*Sir James Jeans, 1937*)[9]

Tonal beauty is an essential – possibly the most essential – technical ideal for all instrumentalists and singers. Though Sir James Jeans' revealing words may dispel some mistaken beliefs about sound production, they can never detract from the essential prerequisite of all practising musicians: the need to consistently strive for beautiful, commanding and magical sounds. No matter how experienced or inexperienced you are as a pianist, and no matter what you are working on, always begin by searching for a specific type of sound. Strive for beauty. The quality of tone you produce at the piano is the key to everything you do.

In searching for beautiful sounds, pianists are battling against two physical truths that are challenging to say the least: firstly, the piano's rapid decay means that it is not possible to *crescendo* on a note after you have played it. Secondly, it uses hammers, which every sensitive artist spends most of their time trying to hide (hammers strike the strings, making true *legato*, something that goes hand in hand with really beautiful tone quality, impossible on the piano).

Wave technique

As we strive towards sonic beauty and purity of tone in our daily practice, it will help if our fingers caress and stroke the keys rather than aggressively hit them. Of course, good teaching traditionally emphasises anti-percussive concepts from the very first lessons.[10] Most of these have already been discussed in

9 From James Jeans' *Science and Music*, Dover Publications Inc., new edition 1969 (ISBN10: 0486619648).
10 This can be seen in many contrasting approaches. Compare the approach of the Russian school with Suzuki teaching and the teaching books of Joan Last. Though the three approaches could not be more contrasted, they are uniform in their insistence on beauty of tone from the first lessons.

The Foundations of Technique, and they include physical *legato* connections (overlaps) between notes as well as the 'touch and press' technique. Pedalling adds another important factor into the equation – one that can radically transform a passage in terms of its sound. Most important of all is the cultivation of relaxed, linear movements. Think in terms of waves and relaxed undulating movements as you play. 'Wave technique' requires physical ease and comfort at the instrument. It encourages greater sensitivity, more *legato* and enhanced beauty of tone. It takes away from the fact that we are striking strings with hammer heads and moves us on to something more evocative and inspirational. By positioning our hands on the keyboard before playing, and either depressing the keys at a 45° angle or drawing our fingers away and towards our bodies as we play, we are immediately setting ourselves up for a sensation of 'lifting' our sounds out of the piano rather than of 'dropping' notes down to the floor. Students who complain that they have insufficient power from 'touching and pressing' at the keyboard compared to attacking the keys from above fail to realise that percussive 'attacked' sounds have a very fast sonic decay. In contrast, sounds produced via relaxed, prepared hands, wave-like arm movements and good coordination have more resonance and carrying power, particularly in large concert halls. Moreover, it becomes much harder to play with clumsy accents and bumps at the ends of phrases when your basic approach at the instrument is tension free! Smooth pianism and elegant contours are simply far easier to produce when your technique works in terms of waves. By developing sound production in this manner from the first lesson, there is immediately a strong sense of connection between player and instrument. The resulting authority, inner intensity and conviction that evolves comes from relaxed, flowing pianism, beginning with sensitive self-listening. It is something that will grow and grow. Of course, sound production is not always about beauty and warmth: the approach outlined would certainly be inappropriate for much of the twentieth- and twenty first-century non-*legato* repertoire. But I strongly believe that the cultivation of beauty of tone is essential for the core repertoire. Thinking and working by searching for beauty in sonority is the most convincing basic starting point for beautiful, healthy and creative piano playing.

Effortless arm movements and relaxed, prepared finger work go hand in hand with pianism and tone inspired by *bel canto* singing. Perhaps no pianist in history was more impressive in this respect than Jan Ignacy Paderewski. With Paderewski's pianism, we are dealing with an artist apparently incapable of producing an ugly sound. Clearly, beauty of tone is one of the most vital ingredients in his art. His use of the *una corda* in *forte* and even *fortissimo* passages would be considered unfashionable in many pedagogical circles today, but the results can be more than magical in the Romantic repertoire from John Field onwards.

Exercises for the development of sound

Pianists of all levels can try simple 'sonority tests' at the piano. These tests help to cultivate the ability to 'float' tone. Depress the sustaining pedal, and then slowly and gently repeat a single note with one finger. Though they need to be executed with fluency, these tests are similar to the exercises in Chapter 12 (p.70) and in Appendix 1 of *The Foundations of Technique*.

Aim for a hollow, disembodied sound as you play. The tone will become more vocally charged and less percussive as you relax into the keyboard. Imagine that the hammers are gently stroking the strings of the note you are playing, rather than attacking them. Slow everything down so that it takes much longer to play a note than you could ever previously have imagined. Let the keys appear to gradually sink into the keyboard on the repetition of each note. Try to avoid percussive, quickly realised re-strikes of keys as you repeat.

Bebung touch

On grand pianos you can aim for a half re-take of the note. Think of this as the 'bebung touch' on the piano.[11] The bebung touch operates on the piano in terms of half escapement and works only on grand pianos. Begin experimenting with bebungs by playing a note *fortissimo* and then quickly re-taking the note in the same finger without lifting the finger off the key. Keep the second note (the repetition of the first) as quiet as possible and try to play it in the same physical movement as the first. It should feel as though the second note is an echo of the first:

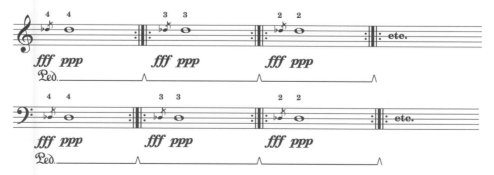

11 Though originally used as a term for a particular approach to touch clavichord playing, Bebung ('trembling') can be applied to piano playing too. In clavichord playing it involves a rocking motion of the finger, moving it up and down on the key in order to create a *vibrato* tone quality.

Leopold Godowsky's pianism embraced extensive use of bebungs for repeated notes; it was one of the hallmarks of his pianism.[12] It is useful to practise the 'bebung effect' on single notes and thirds, and players of all abilities can experiment with the above exercise, extending it to all ranges of the piano and using different fingerings as well as double-note combinations.

Bebungs on the piano are especially useful and expressive for passages containing many veiled repeated notes, such as those in the left hand of Chopin's Prelude in E minor, Op.28 No.4. An editorial note from the old ABRSM Fielden & Craxton edition of this piece recommends 'playing the repeated notes in the left hand with a kind of "bebung" effect, i.e. without the keys coming up to full height, producing a sustained murmuring':

Mastering the bebung touch is extremely useful for developing beauty of tone. It can be applied to all kinds of repertoire and in many different stylistic contexts. It is sad that upright pianos cannot really cope with it, so students who practise regularly on these instruments, or on electronic digital keyboards, need to make a point of specifically practising bebungs whenever they gain access to a grand instrument.

Find the 'sweet spot'

The term 'sweet spot' was originally used in sporting contexts to describe places where a combination of factors results in a maximum response for a given amount of effort.[13] In piano playing, we can think about finding the sweet spot in terms of sound production. Through relaxed coordination and acute listening skills it should be possible for us to find beauty and magic in every note we play. Practising the bebung technique can help us to find the 'sweet spot' for a note, as the repeated notes played with half-retakes of the hammer head often sound disembodied, floaty and ethereal in terms of touch and tone.

Dina Parakhina has often cited Rachmaninov when he suggested that students may enjoy imagining strawberries under their finger pads as they search for beauty of sound. Certainly, the image of graceful movements from each finger in turn, allowing the sweet strawberry juice to gently ooze out over the keyboard, is highly evocative! It inspires students towards a slower, more considered and lovingly sensitive speed of finger articulation for each note.

12 Private conversations with Ronald Stevenson, West Linton, 1990.
13 In cricketing terms, for example, the sweet spot on a bat is the point at which maximum impact can be made by a batsman. If a ball is struck directly from the bat's sweet spot, then the ball will travel further and faster. Other points of impact on the bat will be less effective.

Strawberry juice will not ooze out gently when digital aggression and high-speed movements are prioritised!

So searching for the sweet spot in terms of tonal beauty at the piano is mainly about speed: notes need to be depressed as slowly as possible. In this respect, it may be worthwhile to experiment with flatter finger work. If you want a brilliant, articulate sound then curved fingers can help, but for depth and sonority, a flatter finger position is more effective because it encourages you to slowly stroke rather than quickly poke the keys. I recommend varying the degree to which fingers are curved according to stylistic needs.[14] As the quotation from Sir James Jeans at the beginning of this chapter points out, velocity is the crucial factor in sound production. Articulating notes with a slow physical approach is therefore essential if you are striving for the most beautiful sound possible.

Controlling touch: things that go bump in the night!

Finding immediate focus, energy and coordination at the piano can elude even the most experienced of players. We all know how unsettling it can be to begin a piece and find that half the notes in the opening chord have failed to 'speak' at all. It is also not uncommon to find yourself putting unwanted accents on weak beats and weak parts of beats. Accents, bumps, unexpected silences and uneven jolts can be most disconcerting for both player and listener, yet they are very rarely discussed in textbooks on technique. It can be really unsettling to find that a well-intentioned attempt at *pianissimo* in a relatively easy piece (such as the opening of Debussy's 'Clair de Lune', or even quiet fare as modest as Edward's MacDowell's *To a Wild Rose*) can lead to disaster, with half the notes failing to sound, or at least failing to sound as evenly and carefully as intended. Younger pianists often blame the piano they are playing for poor regulation or an unfamiliar touch, and whilst I would not dispute the fact that no two pianos are the same in this respect, nor question that many pianos are simply not serviced regularly enough to be ideal by concert standards, I do feel that many problems in this area can be solved by focusing on tone production in a specific way. So how can we guarantee that a chord will speak when we depress the keys? How can we avoid a jarring accent in the middle of a *pianissimo* phrase? Being able to control sounds at all times has to be a top priority in building a successful and reliable technique. Let's look at the causes for mishaps – for bumps and blanks, so to speak – and then try to find some practical solutions so that they can be avoided as much as possible.

Lack of control in this sense is caused chiefly by stiffness in the wrists and elbows. It is vital to remain flexible and supple in both, as well as in the shoulders and neck. As noted from the first chapters of *The Foundations of Technique*, firm finger work from the knuckles downwards is an essential

---

14   It is certainly useful to experiment with the position of fingers. Curved fingers may be the norm in Classical and Baroque music, or when clarity and brilliance of tone are priorities, but many find that it is much easier to achieve rich singing pianism in the Romantic repertoire by playing – literally – with flat fingers. Of course, Horowitz was well known for this. The crucial point is a stylistic one, and it is fascinating to vary the curvature of the fingers according to the musical demands presented.

requisite for reliable articulation, but it must be coordinated and synchronised with relaxation in the rest of the body. Of course, wayward instruments with poor regulation can be a law unto themselves, but the odds on controlling sounds are made more favourable when the player is able to adopt a few requisite technical principles that are basic to healthy and reliable pianism at all levels. Begin by preparing notes in advance – never attack the keys from above. This will eliminate percussive sonorities from the tonal palette, ensuring that the arm and body are directly involved in the production of the sound. This is, of course, the 'touch and press' approach, and it immediately ensures that sounds are being controlled by much more than mere fingertip brilliance. If you are feeling uncertain about whether or not notes will speak when you attempt to depress them, it can be helpful to begin this technique with a small upward 'backswing' – keeping the fingers stuck on the keys at all times – so that you have more leverage. At the precise moment the note/s speak, take special care to ensure that your wrists and forearms are in perfect alignment, forming a straight line. Avoid at all costs wrists that stick either upwards or downwards. This is vitally important, as it is only through excellent coordination between wrists and arms that you can be guaranteed control over your playing.

Pianists of all levels can learn to control sound production by practising repeating simple triads in each hand separately. The arm-weight exercise in Appendix 1 of *The Foundations of Technique* (p.114) is a good starting point, but any chord that lies within your hand's natural stretch will do nicely for this purpose.

Once chords can be articulated with confidence so that all the notes speak, it is time to move on to music. There are so many examples that could be chosen to work at, but perhaps one of the most significant with regard to this subject from the standard recital repertoire is the second movement ('Largo e mesto') of Beethoven's Sonata in D major, Op.10 No.3. It has an exceptionally broad tempo and so requires confident control and infallible coordination if bumps and blanks are to be avoided.

Try using concentrated arm movement on every note at first. The 'touch and press' technique will enable beautiful sounds to emerge, and each of the six notes in each chord should sound out with appropriate focus if you try small backswings in your practising as a means towards perfect ensemble playing on each chord. Make sure that your wrists and forearms are in perfect alignment at the point at which the key is depressed fully. Use a mirror to examine where your wrists and arms end up after each quaver is struck.

Chopin's 'Aeolian Harp' Étude in A flat, Op.25 No.1, can be notoriously hard for students to realise effectively. Too often, notes remain silent after they have been played, leaving holes in the texture for the listener and a sense of real bewilderment and frustration for the pianist. It is all too easy to rush over the less-vital arpeggiated accompaniment flourishes in the treble and bass parts of this étude by focusing exclusively on the fifth-finger notes in both hands. Of course, fifth-finger notes are vitally important here, but in order to play the complete texture (rather than omitting literally dozens of notes!) it is essential to listen out when practising for everything.

Try stopping at the end of each bar and using your ears to detect if there are any notes missing in the beautiful chords that you sustain with the pedal after every beat. If you notice holes, then you can concentrate your efforts when practising by using a little arm movement on every single semiquaver. When you have finished working in this way and are ready for a performance, try using the momentum of one single arm movement from each fifth-finger note as you play through every beat in the study. Try to keep your fingers as close as possible to the keyboard. Ideally, you should also adopt the 'touch and press' technique here, along with a subtle rotary movement as the arpeggios gently oscillate.

'Sposalizio', from Liszt's *Années de Pèlerinage* Book 2, shows a much more spartan texture than that of the Chopin étude, but therein lies the problem. Often a shortage of notes means that the player becomes more concerned than ever about mishaps and a lack of control. Bars 1–2 can be mastered by gently swinging from one note to the next with economical but concentrated wrist movements:

Use clockwise rotary movements to firmly navigate your accent-free path down the pentatonically flavoured left-hand fragment. In contrast, bars 3–4 can perhaps best be viewed as a musical sigh. Take the three-note phrases as one-movement gestures from the two five-note chords. Relax, and enjoy sinking into these delicious sounds – the other notes will float effortlessly out from the impact you have created via relaxed, coordinated arm movements.

In the next chapter we will go further into how pianists can technically control all the sounds they produce. There is a gamut of colouristic possibilities open to everyone when they learn to embrace imagination. Aural skills, physical coordination and the internal pre-play of sounds make this possible.

5 Colour

Dynamics

We may play an instrument that has only black-and-white keys, but we are fortunate in the colossal potential it has for tonal variety. A convincing and wide-ranging tonal palette can, and indeed should, be developed from the very first piano lesson. Begin by discovering dynamic levels and thresholds. Firstly, play single notes and triads with up to eight different levels of dynamics:

The aim here is to be as clear and precise with your dynamic differentiations as possible. If you can convincingly project these notes and triads at *ppp*, *pp*, *p*, *mp*, *mf*, *f*, *ff* and *fff*, you will be made aware of your own technical capabilities. This can then be extended to repertoire. Try out the opening phrase of each piece you are currently studying at each of the eight dynamic levels listed. You can then relate the dynamic markings on the score to your own technical abilities. Often it is enough to try out only three or four different dynamic levels in order to gain a sense of tonal perspective and a stronger awareness of your dynamic range. The opening of Schubert's great Sonata in B flat, D.960, is an excellent example:

Try playing it at *mezzo forte* to begin, then repeat it at *piano*, *pianissimo* (the given marking) and finally triple *pianissimo*. Practising regularly in this way will make you more confident in terms of control. You will be more aware of the printed dynamic markings and more conscious of when you are in danger of stepping out of the sound range of the music.

Of course, when you come to perform in public venues it is extremely useful to know your tonal limits: sometimes small or over-resonant venues can be difficult to manage. Trying out a passage at several different dynamic levels can help you to 'zone in' on the most appropriate tonal range for the performance. This is helpful for repertoire and players of all levels.

Experimenting

You can encourage colouristic development in your playing by embracing experimentation in technical work. There is nothing more limiting or uninspiring than refusing to allow beginners the right to enjoy experimenting at the piano – in all its registers. This is easily overcome by simply encouraging scales, exercises and even pieces to be practised at octave ranges different from those suggested on the printed page. Why not?!

Alongside a reluctance to allow students access to the extreme registers of the piano comes an unwillingness to show them how to use the pedals. There seems to have been a widespread myth that pedalling should not be introduced to piano playing until after Grade 5 – despite the fact that many pieces from the earliest grades are impossible to play without pedalling! Happily, things are beginning to change now. The Lang Lang piano method (*Mastering The Piano*, Faber Music[15]) for example, certainly encourages experimentation. Students are allowed to cross hands and pedal freely from the first pages onwards. There are other illuminated tutor books around, notably from Alfred[16], that begin with pieces using only black keys. The point is that pianists of all abilities need to be stimulated and excited by the variety as well as the quality of sounds they are producing. If you limit sound to white-note pitches within an octave of middle C, and do not constantly remember that there are huge possibilities with regard to dynamics, then you risk becoming very uninspired indeed.

Bars 1–13 of the Primo part in Ronald Stevenson's duet *Song for New Year's Day*[17] can be tackled by beginner pianists as they consist of only one chord – but what evocative and inspiring sounds are possible from this single sound:

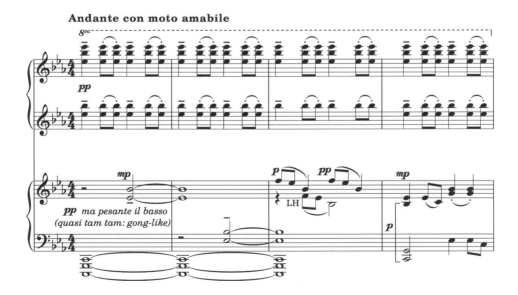

---

15 *Lang Lang Piano Academy: Mastering the Piano Level 1*, Faber Music Ltd (2014).
16 Alfred's Basic Piano Prep Course: lesson book A: William A. Palmer, Morton Manus and Amanda Vick Lethco (Alfred Music).
17 From Two Chinese Folk-Songs for Piano Duet (Ronald Stevenson Society, 2001).

No matter how inexperienced the pianist, the single repeated chord in the Primo here can certainly stimulate tonal variety. Indeed, the possibilities are there for pianists of all abilities to have fun too! The sustaining pedal can be held down for the full duration at first, and then released at various moments. As well as playing the passage at different dynamic levels, the chord can be lifted out of the pedal on each repetition, giving an effect of 'throwing your voice', or 'lifting' sounds out of the piano. As a contrast to this, the hands can remain extremely close to the keyboard. Further variation of tone can be obtained by balancing the left hand more strongly than the right, and vice versa. Inner notes in the chord can be emphasised more strongly than others. The possibilities for variety in sound are almost limitless!

Beyond dynamics

For pianists, the imagination must be engaged in order to develop variety of colour. We look down on a black-and-white collection of keys and find that it is all too easy to depress them consistently in the same way. For this reason, it is vital that you listen regularly to non-piano music. From the first stages of learning the piano to the last, there is a need for stimulation from all the orchestral instruments and the human voice, as well as the organ, lute and guitar. Hearing extra-pianistic sonorities in your head – sounds outside a piano's sound-world – can help to bring new colours to your playing. This has nothing to do with dynamics, but rather with the quality of sound produced from the instrument. It is vital for teachers to insist on an awareness of all the orchestral instruments from their students – from the first lessons. If a pianist is unaware of extra-pianistic sounds, then the colour he or she produces at the piano will be vague. The more awareness and detailed knowledge pianists have about other instruments, the better. It is impossible to over-emphasise this.

Try out different accents and dialects in everyday speech as a means of understanding how you can bring variety of colour to the same material. I often joke that it is not possible to be a convincing pianist unless you are a convincing mimic of other people's voices!

Pianists should imagine themselves as operatic singers and conductors of great orchestras. There will be more on singing from Chapter 6 onwards. Meanwhile, let's explore some of the orchestral qualities inherent in the piano.

Orchestral colours

You are the conductor; your keyboard is the orchestra. Your task is to make every sound that emanates from your fingers as extra-pianistic – or evocative of other instruments – as possible. The ideal repertoire for this experiment is Beethoven's piano sonatas, because each sonata can be considered from the perspective of either a string quartet or a classical orchestra. In working through a section of the 32 sonatas in this manner, try to be as detailed and specific in terms of instrumentation as possible. The slow introduction to Sonata No.26 'Les Adieux', Op.81a, is a good example:

There is not one note of the Beethoven sonatas that cannot be imagined
in terms of orchestral or string-quartet colours. Internalising a complete
movement from Beethoven in terms of instrumental sonority is an inspiring
way to extend your tonal range.

But orchestral pianism should begin in the first lesson. Playing single notes
with different tonal perspectives is something beginners will enjoy exploring.
Later, the imitation of different orchestral instruments should be incorporated
into scale work, exercises, studies and pieces. Allowing your ear to be the
teacher is a surefire way of making progress. As you strive for specific sounds,
and repeat passages in practice, you will find that the shape of your fingers and
the speed at which you depress and release keys changes naturally, without
you being conscious of anything happening. Allow your listening skills to
develop so that they can 'teach' you how to colour.

Here are some excellent examples for practising via self-listening and
repetition. For elementary players, Schumann's *Album for the Young* and Grieg's
Lyric Pieces are very helpful. This phrase from the opening piece, 'Melodie', in
Schumann's *Album for the Young* is extremely useful if approached via tonal
variety in repetitive practice:

Strive to imitate different sounds with repetitions of this phrase. It could be
presented in your imagination as a piece for violin with piano accompaniment.
If you choose to think of it as a piece for flute and piano, then you would
probably adopt a lighter touch for the right hand. If you think of the right hand
as being for recorder, with a guitar playing the left hand, then the tone would
be even less heavy. Alternatively, the piece could be recreated internally for
organ or harpsichord.

Grieg's 'Watchman's Song' (*Lyric Pieces* Book 1, Op.12 No.3) may be well within the range of most Grade 3 players. Its orchestral colours are an essential ingredient in its compositional make-up and need to be projected with conviction. It is easy to imagine a full string orchestra at the opening:

With bars 25–7, trombone pedal points, bassoon arpeggios and upper-woodwind fanfares come to mind:

Scarlatti's sonatas are full of extra-keyboard association and evocation. The Sonata in D major, K.96, begins with a trumpet fanfare that needs extra-curved fingers and fast articulation in order to be appropriately bright and arresting:

From bar 33 of the same sonata, the repeated notes evoke *tremolandos* from a flamenco guitarist and need to be played with appropriate lightness of touch:

Bars 48–52 are more lyrical and could be considered in terms of violins or flutes, according to choice:

When making choices about colours, it is a good idea to mark on the piano score the instruments that come to mind. It is also good to stimulate the imagination by listening to transcriptions of piano works being studied. Some of these may not be in the best possible taste (personally, I always cringe when listening to the exquisite slow movement of Ravel's *Sonatine* played on the alto saxophone!), and many go beyond the scope of the originals in terms of colour (listen, for example, to my own recording with the tenor saxophone player Tommy Smith of Erik Satie's *Gnossienne* No.3[18]), but the point is that knowledge is power. By broadening your awareness of what is possible, you give yourself more possibilities. With this in mind, I encourage students to make up their own transcriptions of piano pieces, especially works that they are currently learning. Transcriptions spring directly from sounds and colours that are imagined internally. Here is the opening of my own arrangement for clarinet (notated at concert pitch) with piano accompaniment of Brahms' Intermezzo in E flat, Op.117 No.1:[19]

Colour and the senses

Beyond our visual and aural imaginations the parameters for inspiration can extend to areas rarely considered, for it is perfectly possible for all our senses – smell, touch and taste – to be utilised in the pursuit of an elevated interpretation. On the subject of taste, it may be the simple physical sensation of eating and drinking that provides inspiration, or perhaps specific tastes. One can draw fascinating parallels between 'biting' chords and 'acidic bitterness', not to mention the effervescent textures of sparkling drinks (Bruno Walter

18 *Gymnopédie: The Classical Side of Tommy Smith* (Linn Records, 1997).
19 This was performed in November 2000 at the RNCM in Manchester by Nicholas Cox and Kathryn Page.

famously described Strauss waltzes as being like 'champagne from Heaven'), 'honeyed' chordal slides or delicate, 'sorbet-like' sonorities.

After smell and taste, touch presents a much more substantive universe of exploration in this respect. Let's look at the finale of Beethoven's E major Sonata, Op.109, as a means of testing approaches that could lead to variety of colour. It goes without saying that in timeless masterpieces there are all kinds of possibilities, and of course inspiration can and should work on many levels. Nonetheless, Beethoven's theme makes physical sense when related to the act of slowly sinking into a deliciously soft pillow stuffed with the finest feathers.

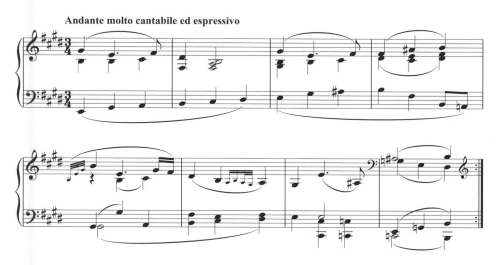

For **Variation 1**, it is compelling to imagine dark, deep velvet (rather than plastic makeshift ivory) as one strokes the keys.

Variation 2 is plucked rather than struck:

The fire and energy in **Variation 3** is very much to the fore as the left hand scampers in childlike mischief away from authoritarian paternal decrees in the right hand:

With **Variation 4**, it is vital to feel gently lifted in undulating waves, albeit at a relatively low height:

One can continue this approach into the final stages of the movement, in which case the quasi-choral Baroque heroics of **Variation 5** need a sense of resonant glow from the diaphragm:

Finally, **Variation 6** lifts the performer upwards to the spiritual heights as never portrayed in keyboard literature before. The climax evokes the sounds of the angels as the piano produces extraordinary trills and resonance (bars 14–17). The acoustics and dimensions of a great cathedral are implied as the music rises higher and higher:

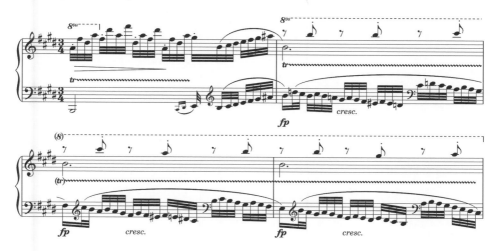

Synaesthesia

Bringing together the senses, known as synaesthesia, is of vital significance when discussing colour and piano playing. Pitch–colour synaesthesia is particularly stimulating for students, not only when studying composers who wrote specifically about their own particular key–colour associations (such as Scriabin and Messiaen), but also for understanding and developing an imaginative response to music in general. In order to continue our quest to transform monochromatic sonority into glorious technicolor, try playing a selection of chords in different keys. Is there a change in atmosphere from one pitch centre to another? For me, personally, sharper keys become brighter, fresher and more energised. G major is the key of springtime, vigour and early-morning forest dew. The G major French Suite of J.S. Bach is entirely representative of this key at its most vibrant and natural. Flatter keys become richer, luxuriant, and almost decadent in mood. When hearing the opening slow arpeggiated chords of Chopin's A flat Nocturne, or the beautiful theme of Beethoven's 'Funeral March' Sonata in A flat, Op.26, I immediately feel more lazy, stretched out and in need of extremely rich chocolate! Surroundings seem to become darker and warmer, as though we have stepped in from nature's realm where the sharper keys seem to reside.

There is a world of difference between playing Schubert's G flat Impromptu, Op.90 No.3, in the original key and playing it in the re-published key of G major.[20]

---

20 Apparently Schubert's publishers were concerned that six flats would stop sales of the piece so insisted that he republish in G major. Happily, we only rarely hear the latter version in performances today.

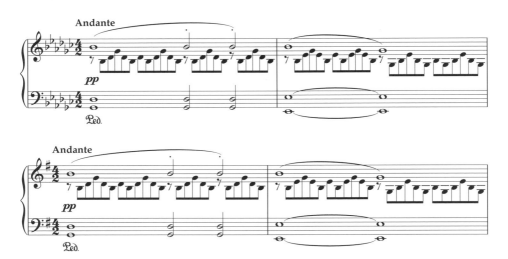

It seems obvious that the key change from G flat major to G major in this famous piece makes the character much less reflective. It turns an introspective piece into something much more energised and bright. Key–colour–mood association becomes particularly fascinating when one plays a piece such as Chopin's Waltz in G flat, Op.70 No.1, which evokes the quality of sharps rather than the notated flats in one's inner ear. I could not even begin to consider the outer sections of this piece – which I see in brilliant 'sunshine' yellow – in G flat major! I need to perceive it in F sharp major, adjusting all the accidentals accordingly, simply because it is clearly a sparkling, effervescent fresh mood that has to be projected (qualities my own peculiar synaesthesia could never associate with a flat key).

Bedding the keys

Progress can be made in a technical way with colour by focusing on concrete physical issues as well as imaginative ones. We can teach colour in a down-to-earth way and make progress with concrete physical possibilities. There are specific technical means by which pianists can learn to vary their tonal range. In terms of sound production, many teachers have strong views: 'dig like a miner' and 'press down deeply with your fingers to the wood below the keys' are battle cries that many will be familiar with. Chapter 8 of *The Foundations of Technique* discusses firm articulation. The production of rich tone at the piano depends on solid digital follow-through, and this is something that can be gradually controlled and mastered through daily work, not only in repertoire but also in scales. Even Hanon exercises can be divorced from high finger work and used as effective means of exploring deep-toned pianism or finger work that reaches down to the bottom of each key bed. Slow, deliberate practice is essential here, leading to an awareness of just how deep the key bed actually is!

The concept of full-blooded articulation cannot be over-stressed. Or can it? The trouble is that we can become obsessed with ideology. Nothing will annoy certain pedagogues more than sloppy finger work. In the early stages in cultivating virtuosity, much of the groundwork that needs to be explained when new students appear with technical difficulties, and many of the day-to-day warm-up concerns of students who are technically well set-up, revolve around this vital approach.

Alongside basic work on strong articulation should come an awareness of the possibilities of touch that need to be developed on shallower levels. Quite simply, our beloved instrument will most certainly 'speak' well before its keys are fully depressed to the bottom of the keyboard, and this fact has, by some in the past, been seen as a tremendous pitfall. Woe betide those pianists who are simply too 'lazy' to bother travelling those extra, vital few millimetres 'downwards', for it is that vital descent that makes all the difference between a Richter and a Joe Bloggs!

When variety of tone becomes a priority, this obsession with full-on key-bedding becomes very unhelpful. It is possible to play *leggiero* music only by depressing the keys partially. The opening of the slow movement of Chopin's Concerto No 2 in F minor immediately comes to mind as an example of music that will only truly shine with a touch that gently kisses and superficially tickles the keys. To go for a full-blown embrace at the bottom of each key would ruin the magic of the filigree here:

I recommend an exploration of key-bedding not only at the deepest and most shallow levels, but also at moderate levels of key depression. This can be seen in the final section of Liszt's 'Mephisto Waltz' No.1 (bars 683–6). The right-hand figurations are too cumbersome if fully bedded, yet too 'music-box like' if tickled superficially:

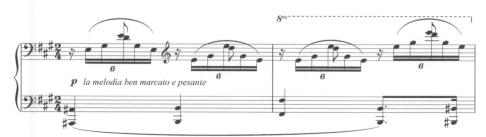

Sonority tests

Let's continue with some basic exercises in order to get started and put varied key-bedding into operation. These can be utilised at all levels. Firstly, a warm-up sonority test: depress the sustaining pedal, and then place your fifth finger of the right hand over the C above middle C. Relaxing your entire arm, begin by gently and comfortably making circular down–up, down–up movements from your wrist as your fingertip remains permanently stuck on the key surface. As the wrist travels down at a 45° angle and then up in the manner of a slow-motion yo-yo, you should feel that your entire being is involved in a beautiful and graceful ritual. No sounds will emerge, but as you gradually increase the intensity of what you are doing and focus on coordination, the key will eventually be allowed to 'speak'. Keep up your intensity of approach with the pedal still depressed, and notice how you achieve an entire gamut of contrasted colours as the key slowly descends to the bottom of its bed. Then try reducing the intensity gradually until you are back at silence. What you have just achieved is remarkable: you will have discovered that there are at least four different levels of key-bedding, all with their own unique colour/characterisation, and all with their specific uses for interpretation at your disposal. You can readily see the possibilities of 'conscious key layering' by looking at the side of the key immediately next to the one you are depressing (the academics amongst us could even measure out the number of millimetres that quantify each stage of key descent!). We can imagine ourselves as divers, explorers of the vast oceanic universe that is the piano. How wrong, then, to limit ourselves to the, admittedly impressive, bottom of the seabed (Level 4) when there are so many delights to celebrate near the surface (Level 1) and just beyond that (Level 2), as well as near the bottom, if not quite on it (Level 3).

Key bedding
Level 1: Surface articulation (playing as lightly as possible)
Level 2: Moderately light articulation
Level 3: Solid articulation
Level 4: Bedding the keys as deeply as possible

Extend this one-note sonority test by trying it with two notes (3rds, 4ths and 5ths), then three (triads of all sorts), and finally with four-note chords in each hand – separately then together. It makes for an excellent aural and physical warm-up and will immediately focus your inner ear creatively on tone. Then experiment with five-finger exercises played at four different key levels. Next, follow this with scales, arpeggios and broken chords. It will be as though you have to totally overhaul your technique, but the creative buzz you will get from the ability to change tone via technique rather than via instinct will certainly stop any resentment being felt. Get into the habit of experimenting with all the sounds in your repertoire by playing at different key levels. By so doing, you are simply mixing colours on your proverbial palette before deciding on the depth of tone you wish to adopt at any given moment for any specific context.

Applying key-bedding techniques to repertoire

Perhaps it is easiest to begin with the repertoire you are currently studying. Never feel that you have to consistently stick to decisions, though. Choices have to be made, but on any given occasion an individual may choose to alter dramatically what has been done previously. Eventually, much will be done quickly, even unconsciously, but for the moment it is useful to 'pin colours to the mast', with the proviso that the colours are only possibilities.

The above example is from Mozart's B flat Sonata, K.570. In bar 1, try a deeper approach for the left hand than for the right (Level 3 as opposed to Level 2), but ensure that the right-hand quavers throughout the passage have sufficient presence and projection without becoming overly heavy (i.e. Level 2). The semiquavers from bar 12 onwards should sparkle and buzz with excitement and joy at Level 1.

Next, some Debussy: the eighth étude *Pour Les Agrèments* from book two of *Douze études*:

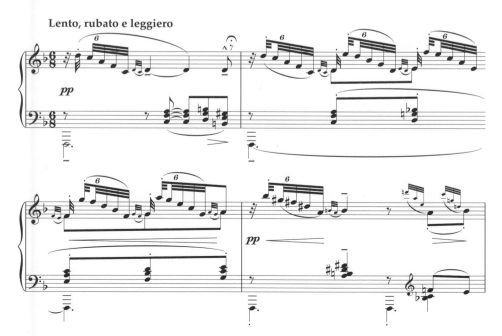

Starting with bar 1, try Level 4 for the low bass Fs. It will be apparent that deep bedding does not imply *fortissimo*, and that every dynamic and articulative approach is possible at each level. Try Level 1 for the light *staccato* D in the right hand of the opening bar, then move down from Level 1 through to Level 3 as you play the ornamental flourish that follows, resting on the first-inversion triads in the left hand. In the second bar, the left-hand triads seem convincing at Level 2, whilst in bar 3 the dominant-seventh 'surprise' chord would imply Level 1. The right-hand sequences in bar 2 begin as in bar 1, but as the intensity increases, so too will the degree of key depression. Again, I stress that this has nothing to do with 'loudness' as such, even though there is an obvious *crescendo* here.

Finally, let's consider Liszt's 'Mazeppa' from his *Transcendental Études* – a classic case of outsized virtuosity in which the pianist would appear to need four rather than two hands in order to cope!

The outer chordal parts work well at the deepest level, though some may prefer to allow the right hand more of a sparkle, bringing a glistening reverberation via Levels 2 or 3 to the texture. The inner double-note stave is clearly a less heavy phenomenon, requiring an approach from Levels 1 or 2. But a word of caution: passages like this require steely finger work, with tremendous firmness from the bridge of the hand. Level 1 does not imply a lack of finger strength. Indeed, it is arguably more difficult to have strong digits in Levels 1 and 2 (where control is extremely difficult) than at Levels 3 and 4.

Physical pre-play

In order to convert your internal musical wishes for variety of colour into
reliability at the keyboard, physical preparation in the split second or so before
you play each note is essential. This can most easily be seen when observing
a fine conductor at work with a world-class orchestra. The huge variety of
gesture and encyclopaedic range of expression implied by a great maestro's
breathing, eyes, body language and speed of delivery all have profound effects
on the sounds that are automatically produced by the orchestra immediately
after each move or impetus from the rostrum. I firmly believe that pianists
can learn a tremendous amount from this. It is not enough to simply remain
relaxed and free and then hope that focus and clarity of sound will result
by vaguely depressing the keys and hoping for success. In order to generate
sufficient conviction, coordination and will power at the instrument we must
focus in advance of every sound we make. Here are three examples of pre-play:

1 The opening of Beethoven's celebrated 'Moonlight' sonata No.14, Op.27 No.2,
   can cause great anxiety and stress if you are not fully engaged and focused
   immediately before you play each triplet quaver:

As the melody of the movement enters, several bars after this opening,
it is essential to internally hear the requisite veiled, disembodied and
ghostly colours required in advance of execution, and then to sense in your
fingertips the energy required to play as your inner ear has suggested. It can
help to adopt flatter finger shapes for the right hand, so that you are playing
with the optimum amount of flesh, turning your fingertips into larger 'pads'
for each note. Flatter fingers will certainly make it easier to play in a muted,
unobtrusive way. Meanwhile, the left-hand octaves give an ominous, dark
and distantly menacing aura to the texture and need a different approach.
Imagine double basses and cellos playing an octave apart. As with the right-
hand quavers, it is important not to over-play their projection, and it is vital
to 'feel' and even draw in your imagination a particular shape for the fingers
to realise when they play each octave. I recommend that the lower note of
each octave (the double-bass part) is given more weight than the top, and it
can help to imagine an infrared light beaming down from your shoulder and
powering into your fifth-finger fingertip, energising it into coordination and
perfect balance for each octave.

2 One of the main challenges in Chopin's *Berceuse*, Op.57 is sustaining a
   consistent and reliable *piano* and *pianissimo* whilst allowing all the notes to
   speak clearly:

At the same time, there is a need for a variety of colour-shading within the hushed overall dynamic level. As with the Beethoven 'Moonlight' sonata, the very opening can seem the most troublesome part of the piece: setting up the rocking rhythm and coming to terms with the held A flat on the second quaver of each left-hand dotted-crotchet beat requires conviction and consideration. It is all too easy to 'hit' these A flats, so it's worthwhile taking time in the split second before they are realised to pre-play them, positioning your finger (I use the fourth, as it is the most sensitive and delicate in the hand) and feeling in advance a sensation of lovingly stroking the key towards your body. Imagine a horn player gently intoning this note as a far distant pedal point. The colour has to be distinct yet unobtrusive. This is achieved through a firmness and sense of solidity in the fingertip: if you are too 'flabby' and out of focus, then you risk a clumsy bump on these notes or, perhaps worse, a 'blank' in which the note fails to sound at all.

3   The final example of pre-play comes from Debussy's 'Reflets dans l'eau' from *Images* (Book 1). As with the Beethoven and Chopin examples above, the challenge is to find pianistic focus for your conception immediately, which must be in sympathy with the extraordinarily intense, inward, dreamlike and hypnotically captivating atmosphere created by the composer:

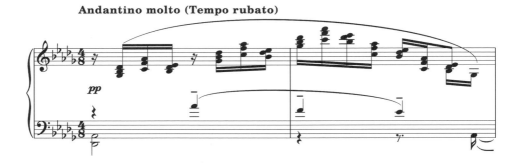

The three descending notes in the tenor register played by the left hand (A flat, F and E flat) have been described by commentators as three pebbles that drop into a still lake, resulting in a whole series of ripples. It is easy to imagine them being played by a clarinettist. Use only your second left-hand finger for them, and try to create 'reverb' and richness via touch that goes deep and 'beds' the keys before rising upwards and letting the sound ring around the hall. In order to ensure that notes are lifted out, rather than continuing to remain embedded, they need to be executed with speed and graceful coordination. As with the left-hand A flats in the Chopin *Berceuse*, the touch adopted involves drawing the hand towards the body, though in this case the arm should lift the hand higher. It can help to imagine that your second finger is weaving a spider's web from its finger pad as you play. The web grows as you lift each note out of the keyboard. As your second finger rises and falls to play the three notes, imagine the web being created everywhere your finger moves. Again, you need to pre-play and pre-hear this touch in the split second before you play each note.

What makes this passage especially challenging is the fact that the chordal semiquavers that surround the three notes need to be kept firmly in the background, whilst the opening low fifth in the left hand needs to have a commanding presence, but without too much heaviness or projection that would take away from the importance of the three 'pebble' notes when they enter. Imagine the semiquavers being realised by the full string section of a symphony orchestra, with harps added into the mix. The fifths could be realised convincingly by muted lower brass, mixed with colour from the timpani. Experimentation and practice via intense listening and repeated attempts will ensure success – provided that the fingers are made aware of the shapes they need to find themselves in immediately before executing each note. Without preparatory focus and consideration in advance of the sound quality required for each note, the success or failure of performance in this repertoire becomes uncertain, appearing to depend more on chance and good fortune than on awareness and purpose of approach.

A colouring list

Although there is no substitute for using your ears to differentiate colours in practice sessions, it may be helpful to conclude this chapter with some down-to-earth practical tips. Here, in broadly alphabetical order, is a colouring list containing a crude selection of seventeen technical approaches that can be used to draw out orchestral and instrumental colours from the piano. Players of all abilities can benefit from this kind of experimentation, provided they are prepared to experiment with curiosity and patience. As with all practising, repetition and self-review are crucial. Make sure that you remain as objective as possible when working through these possibilities. If you find it difficult to judge how successful you are at evoking specific colours from your instrument, enlist the help of a listener or use an electronic device. Eventually, you should develop sufficient self-awareness to cope with experimentation entirely through the use of your own ears alone.

Cello You need to dig down to the bottom of the key bed in order to emulate the glorious resonance of a cello. Use full arm weight and celebrate richness and resonance with full glory.

Clarinet Enjoy playing from the finger pads with a flatter than normal finger shape. Level 3 in terms of key-bedding would be most appropriate, as the sounds are rich without being excessively heavy.

Double bass As with the cello sound, you need to dig down as deeply as possible here. The string family all have a similar approach in terms of technique, and differences of sound will come naturally from the particular register in which a passage is written. With 'double bass' colours, listen intently to the reverberation of notes after you have struck them ('struck' being a rather insensitive word to use, of course!). Be acutely aware of the vibrations/beats. This resonance and afterglow is especially useful in recreating a sense of string sonority. Double-bass *pizzicato* can be convincingly recreated at the piano by quickly 'flicking off' bass notes and ensuring that no pedal whatsoever is employed.

Flute Light and transparent sounds are easier to produce if you play on the surface (Level 1) of the keys rather than with deep finger work. Fingers should be slightly, but not overly, curved. There should be a firmness of touch, but it should be cultivated with an awareness of delicacy. Avoid accentuation at all costs.

Guitar There is an immediacy about the tone of the guitar. Try to capture the sharp, brusque immediacy of a flamenco player's *rasgueados* ('strumming') technique by playing with fast-flicking finger work (see pp.34–5 of *The Foundations of Technique*). Curve your fingers consciously so that they become energised, sharp and decisive. This touch should be executed on the surface (Level 1) of the keyboard. Clearly, speed and agility are of paramount importance here.

Harp Harps are much more reverberant than guitars. They are also less agile and as a consequence require a more stroking touch – use flatter fingers than in the guitar touch. Stroke the keys towards your body and listen to the afterglow of each note. Level 3 in terms of key-bedding would seem the most appropriate.

Harpsichord Clarity of articulation is the main requirement. Curve you fingers and avoid excessive overlaps between notes. Try bedding the keys at Level 2.

Horn Horns are commanding but not aggressive in tone quality. To evoke their majesty you need firm fingers with lots of relaxed weight behind them. Bedding the keys to the third or even fourth level would seem appropriate, as would use of arm weight. The edgy quality associated with horn tone could be impersonated via a fast-moving attack for each note as it is articulated. But this has to be balanced with relaxation and ease of movement from the wrists and arms in order to prevent sonorities from becoming too aggressive.

Marimba The marimba has a woolly, relaxed, rather unclear sonority. There is little brilliance to the tone. Adopt flatter fingers here and play at Level 2. Avoid being either too heavy or too light.

Organ Overlap your finger work as much as possible in order to recreate the enormous resonance and deep glow associated with the organ. Use Level 4 and play with full arm weight. Keep fingers as close to the keys as possible.

Recorder This requires a similar approach to that used for flute sounds, but with still more delicacy. The touch can be even lighter and less firm. It is contrasted from attempts to emulate the piccolo in that recorder playing is always less piercing and reverberant. The speed with which notes are depressed can help to differentiate flute, recorder and piccolo sounds. Try to show a clear difference between the three.

Timpani The timpani has a commandingly big sound. However, the initial attack on each note from the timpani tends to be rather muted. Use flatter fingers but dig down deep (Level 4) into the key bed. The afterglow of a timpani's resonance is crucial. Release sounds with your fingers whilst retaining the sustaining pedal. As you let go of each note, imagine that your fingertip is still connected to keyboard surface by a spider's web (or chewing gum if you prefer!).

Triangle and xylophone The afterglow of brilliant resonance is crucial here. Release notes as fast as possible, using the pedal and experimenting with Levels 2 and 3 rather than aiming to bed the keys. The initial impetus for each note should also be taken at a mercurial speed. Do not wait around on the key bed longer than you have to, though the triangle touch should be a little shorter than the xylophone one.

Trumpet Aim for a strong, almost metallic sound here. Brilliance and sharp finger work are the priorities. Curve your fingers as much as possible and play at Level 2 or 3. Lift your fingers up and strive for clarity at all costs. Try to avoid clipping the ends of notes by listening fully after depressing the keys.

Trombone and tuba Differences in register will naturally convert horn and trumpet sonorities into trombone and tuba colours. Bass-register passages that work well in terms of brass instruments tend to be forceful, clear and incisive. You can cultivate these qualities by ensuring that your fingers remain curved rather than flat. Aim for Levels 2 or 3 in terms of key-bedding and avoid excessive overlapping between notes.

Violin The approach taken in the cello touch applies here, though violins have more immediate intensity than cellos and use faster vibrato. A pianist therefore needs to adopt a faster approach to articulation when attempting to emulate a violin's resonance. Use Level 4 in the key-bedding hierarchy. There should be a firmness in the fingertips at all times – a sense of soloistic command – so that the sounds have as much definition and dominance as possible.

Viola The viola touch requires a halfway house between the violin and cello approaches outlined above. The darker, expressive melancholy of the viola requires a deep, rich tone (Level 4) but without the full weight and resonance of a cello. Vibrato is slightly slower than on the violin, so the speed with which your fingers articulate notes can be a little less energised.

6 Sounds: horizontal development

Chapters 4 and 5 were concerned mainly with sounds in isolation. Let's now introduce techniques that bring notes together. Connecting sounds into musical units leads naturally into discussions on phrasing and structure, but this chapter begins with a consideration of vocal influences. All pianists need to know how to make the instrument sing and speak. They need to be able to breathe as they play in order to master the crucial techniques of *cantabile* and *parlando*.

Melodic intervals

We all know that each interval has its own peculiar emotional characteristics, whatever period it comes from. Yet it is surprising how often pianists can take melodic jumps for granted, forgetting to emotionally engage in, say, a strikingly expressive major-sixth ascent after a melodic progression in steps.[21] This is one of the reasons why pianists should never shy away from singing. As soon as the vocal aspect of a pianist's musicianship is neglected, phrasing and beauty of tone become much harder to achieve. It is not for nothing that piano teachers of stature often love to warble their way through hour after hour of piano lessons, much to the amusement of their students. But if it helps to cement a real understanding of *moto espressivo* via intervallic awareness, then their efforts are certainly not misplaced.

Singing and speaking: *cantabile* and *parlando*

Cantabile ('singing', or 'in a singing style') and *parlando* (indicative of expressive declamation, suggestive of speech) go hand in hand in pianism that emphasises lyrical and expressive phrasing. For instrumentalists, they imply a relaxed, authoritative approach at the opposite end of the spectrum from playing that parallels tense, nervous shouting. *Cantabile* and *parlando* make performers worth listening to. There is no question that a pianist who can emulate something of the expressivity, warmth and beauty that is usually evident in the voices, performances and speeches of the greatest singers and orators will be an artist rather than just an instrumentalist.

When Beethoven wrote the direction 'con una certa espressione parlante' in his sixth *Bagatelle* from the Op.33 set, he was emphasising the need for the performer to seek a parallel with the art of oratory. The starting point in this exploration has to be a connection with vocal declamation and delivery. If pianists cannot speak expressively, or at least have an inner conception of how they wish to convey words, sentences, paragraphs, and so on, it is very hard for them to play expressively. For words, substitute notes; for sentences,

---

21 For a full and fascinating examination of this subject, see Deryck Cooke's important study *The Language of Music* (Oxford University Press, 1959).

phrases. Just as it is important to breathe naturally as you speak, to colour with feeling the message you are presenting, so it is in music. Whether you speak in French, German or in music, you need to have a clear grasp of microstructure and macrostructure; the ability to move towards key words; a real warmth and belief in the message you are communicating; and a natural ease in delivery that will make your voice sound relaxed and effortless, rather than hard-edged and uncomfortable. It is fascinating to listen to recordings of politicians who were great orators, such as Winston Churchill and Michael Foot, and to remember that one of the most expressive pianists of all time, Paderewski, also had a career as the President of Poland! For an example of exquisite *cantabile* and *parlando* on disc, Paderewski's extremely free but always beautiful performance of Chopin's F sharp Nocturne (on Pearl, *Paderewski plays Chopin*) remains a particularly expressive and magical achievement, despite the primitive quality of the sound engineering.

Shading

Tonal shading – miniscule but sensitively delivered variations in dynamics – is a vital necessity for *cantabile* and *parlando* playing on the piano. Phrases that remain at one dynamic level sound machine-like and empty, and it is the performer's responsibility to constantly project subtle but clear inflexions of tone – i.e. to shade – so that the melodic line becomes a multicoloured phenomenon rather than a monochrome series of pitches. However, shading needs to be used with great caution, for indiscriminate and extreme *crescendos* followed by *diminuendos* can make a pianist's phrasing sound just as mechanical and predictable as phrasing with no changes in dynamics. Sincerity is often the bedfellow of simplicity here, and the vocal parallel is to think of a television presenter who is too eager to exaggerate key phrases as they read out the banalities of their autocue!

Weight transfer

Cantabile and *parlando* are impossible without sensitive listening and lots of trial and error in the rehearsal studio. In *The Foundations of Technique* we discussed 'touch and press' technique. A beautiful sound can also be developed by stroking the keys towards your body as you play. Both 'touch and press' and stroking the keys encourage *cantabile* playing, but its cultivation is stimulated even more when you are able to transfer weight effortlessly. This should be done in a melodic line with relaxed, graceful movements from one note to the next. Use graceful, focused and economical wave-like movements from the wrist. A very inspiring and helpful exercise for this, recommended by the late Yonty Solomon,[22] is to take a melodic line and play all of its notes with the third finger only. Gently place the tip of your thumb behind it and move from one note in a phrase to the next with graceful undulating movements.

22   Lessons at the Royal College of Music in London with Kathryn Page.

Let's apply this to Bach's famous Minuet in G (BWV 114) from the 'Anna Magdalena' notebook:

The effect should look and feel as though you are elegantly painting with a light brush as you move from one note to the next. The use of the third finger alone in this manner promotes consistency and evenness. It also encourages you to strive for accent-free phrasing, which is vital for *cantabile*. You can then return to conventional fingering in the chosen phrase – and find that everything flows much more vocally and eloquently. Relaxation remains the vital aspect here, as well as coordination. But most important of all is the ability to listen carefully.

Vocalisation: the simplest step towards natural phrasing

With ensemble singing becoming less and less a part of contemporary school life, it can be difficult to encourage students to sing phrases from a piece of music out loud in lessons. But singing is a fundamental part of western music and is key to understanding how music flows. Of course, inspiration from and imitation of the human voice has been considered important in instrumental playing for centuries. One needs only to look briefly at well-known treatises on playing musical instruments from the first half of the eighteenth century to see this – e.g. books by C.P.E. Bach (keyboard instruments), Leopold Mozart (violin) and Quantz (flute). And it has long been standard practice for teachers to encourage their keyboard students via 'singing through the fingers'. An emulation of a great vocalist's sense of line and awareness of shape is important for inspiration and guidance in most of the standard non-percussive piano repertoire. But before you start to work consciously at phrasing and structure, try out the simple technique of vocalisation: begin by singing out loud a phrase that you are about to play, without preparation. It does not matter about the quality of your voice. Simply enjoy the melodic shape you are singing. Repeat the process for as long as it takes for you to feel really confident about the direction and mood of the phrase in question. Finally, play the phrase on the piano in exactly the same way as you have been singing it. This is what I call vocalisation at the piano. If you are unsure about your singing, record yourself and listen back; experiment with different approaches, and then return to the keyboard. The difference in what you are doing will usually be both obvious and exciting. Ultimately, vocalisation needs to be distilled so that you learn to 'sing internally' as you play. This is vital for creating a convincing *cantabile* in all kinds of melodic contexts. If there is no clear inner conception, there can be no sense of shape and certainly therefore little hope of achieving pianism evocative of the human voice.

Bowing for pianists

As well as gaining inspiration for phrasing from singers, pianists can learn a lot from their string-playing colleagues. Even the slightest awareness of down- and up-bows can prove invaluable when a keyboard player is searching for ways to articulate and shape music. This is especially true for music in the pre-Beethoven era, where printed pages are often spartan, with nothing on them apart from the notes themselves. Clearly, for eighteenth-century composers the printed text was a much smaller part of the completed compositional picture than it was for composers from the nineteenth century, who included a significantly greater amount of information in their compositions. Of course, the principles of bowing should be used in music of all periods, but it seems particularly basic and essential in Baroque and early- Classical music because of the incomplete nature of the printed texts. Bowing can help us to avoid performing Bach with consistent *staccato* (the 'woodpecker' effect) or, at the other extreme, playing it with a seamlessly consistent *legato* (turning everything into a proverbial organ work). Though both of these extreme approaches can work, for the vast majority of compositions by J.S., J.C. and C.P.E. Bach, Handel, Telemann, Scarlatti, Cimarosa, Clementi, Haydn and Mozart (etc.!), mixed articulation is far more natural. There are so many possibilities with bowing. The variety that comes from thinking through music as a bowing string player rather than as a pianist will consistently refresh your musical punctuation and sense of shape.

So how does it work? Up-bows (⋁) on the piano translate as lighter, lifted gestures. Obviously, upbeats, weak beats and offbeats work best when articulated as up-bows. You can have several up-bows in succession when you wish to pontificate, keep music in suspense and/or delay the resolution of a cadence or pivotal note in a phrase (subtly or otherwise). This can be seen in the first three quavers of the D major fugue subject from Book 2 of Bach's *The Well-Tempered Clavier*:

Pianistic up-bow gestures include movements that take the hands up and away from the keyboard. There is an enormous range of possibilities in terms of upward direction of movement: either drawing your hands towards your body, or lifting them up in a perpendicular way, or 'flicking' your fingers outwards as described in Chapter 6 of *The Foundations of Technique*. Up-bow gestures also vary in terms of tempo. As shown in the following three examples, you can make them slow and lusciously expansive (*Brahms*); flirtatious or angry (*Mozart*); or fast (*Beethoven*):

Brahms: Intermezzo in A, Op.118 No.2

Mozart: Sonata in A major, K.331, finale

Beethoven: Sonata in C minor, Op.111

Indeed, the whole gamut of emotional characterisation comes into play when you begin to 'bow' your piano music! Down-bows are more assertive, definite and anchoring than up-bows. Their emphatic, positive nature makes them essential for strong beats and accents, and also for stamping the hallmark of confidence and strength at the beginning of a technical flourish. The sense of a down-bow's attack on the first note of a run can give you the energy to take all the notes in the flourish in one physical gesture. This can be seen in the soloist's first entry in the first movement of Beethoven's Piano Concerto No.3:

As with up-bows, down-bows can make use of an enormous range of different touches. As well as rapid single-movement thrusts (as in the Beethoven Concerto above), you can sink more lazily into the keyboard. You can also employ all the different levels of key-bedding as described in Chapter 4. Sharp, percussive attack can work equally well as an up- or down-bow, as can 'touch and press' technique, though here the effect of bowing will be more psychological or mental and less literal, as the gestures of moving a bow are not physically reproduced. I recommend that at some stage you look at all your music in these terms.

Marking into the score a range of possible bowings can be extremely revealing. Let's close this section by taking the opening of Bach's A minor Two-Part Invention No.13 BWV 784 and marking in two alternative possibilities for 'bowing' (there are of course an infinite number of possibilities):

Example 1

Example 2

Words and music

Another technique that is useful for encouraging musical shaping is potentially amusing, and even rather mischievous if taken too far: composing words to fit musical motifs and phrases. This has a long history in piano playing. Apparently Liszt used to write lines of poetry beneath the notes in his students' music, whilst Harold Craxton was known for adopting very amusing words in various contexts! Here are some words by Busoni to the second famous subject in the first movement of Mozart's Concerto in C major, K.467:

Busoni's illuminating choice of words[23] immediately gives both shape and sensitive characterisation to the phrasing, encouraging the pianist towards increased intensity at the repetition of the words 'Lasz mich' and towards a real sense of impassioned wonder at the top of the rising-sixth interval and the word 'Leben'. The pianist is immediately inspired to think in extra-pianistic terms and to focus his or her awareness of shape, mood and direction in keeping with singing and the – appropriately emotional – words.

If you can find suitable words and say them out loud as you practise, your rhythmic direction and sense of direction in phrases cannot fail to be convincing. Use this method for the most basic rhythmic cells (for example, for three triplet quavers try saying 'mer-ri-ly' or 'straw-ber-ry') as well as for motifs in big movements (try saying 'Oh woe is me' for the obsessive four-note pattern that appears at the beginning of the finale in Beethoven's 'Tempest' Sonata, Op.31 No.2):

This opening three-note motif is obsessively prevalent throughout the movement, and the chosen words can help players in terms of melodic shape, character and focus. It may be amusing to sing them out loud in practice, but it is also beneficial and inspirational, preventing the music from rushing and becoming too breathless.

Composing words to extended phrases is useful in all kinds of contexts. What about the following, attributed to the late Sydney Harrison,[24] for help with direction and characterisation in the second subject of Tchaikovsky's Piano Concerto No.1 (first movement):

23 Excerpt from Busoni's essay 'The Score of Doktor Faust', reprinted in *The Essence of Music and other Essays*.
24 From private conversations with Norma Fisher, London, 1989.

It is also is fascinating and instructive to study transcriptions of songs for solo piano, and to try to sing out loud the original words for the song as you play the melodic line at the keyboard. When playing arrangements of songs as piano solos we are in essence becoming storytellers and actors as well as singers and accompanists. It is vital that the vocal lines from the original songs are projected over the accompaniment parts with sufficient conviction and intensity so that listeners unfamiliar with the original songs can still follow and understand the melodic shapes and contours as something independent from the accompaniment textures. Interpretation becomes at once more straightforward as well as more challenging as the pianist attempts to follow and 'paint' the words of song transcriptions through his or her fingers, drawing the listener into the – often explicit – narrative of the mood of the music. Quite often the tempo of the original song will need to be adjusted in order to manage the complexities of the arrangement, but this is all part of the challenge and stimulation that working with Liszt's 'commentaries' on lieder can bring.

Here is an extract (bars 4–7) from Liszt's celebrated transcription of the Schumann Song 'Widmung':

The words give immediate direction to the vocal line (note that the high F in the top line has the pivotal word 'joy'), but there are challenges aplenty with the repeated Cs in the first bar here and, more generally, with regard to projecting convincingly the vocal line over the lower figurations. This extract requires much experimentation in the practice room, with repetitions and constant adjustments to tone and tonal balance before conviction can emerge.

Before going any further it makes sense to take stock by applying some of the main ideas explored in this chapter to slower, expressive and melodic pieces from the repertoire you are currently studying. When you approach a piece in which the melodic line is all-important, imagine that you are singing, breathing and thinking about the score from a vocal perspective. If it helps, add words to the melodic line. Colour, direction of line and shaping on a small and large scale are everything here: you are attempting to emulate the vocal ideal at the keyboard. To do this, your practice session should comprise a mixture of literal and internal singing. As with all good practice, self-listening remains of paramount importance, but it can be far easier to focus on the task in hand if the atmosphere of an operatic stage is not only visualised but actually felt.

Words and rhythmic coordination

Words can be used for technical–rhythmic coordination when dealing with isometric rhythmic patterns. So often when amateur pianists attempt to play in triplets in one hand and duplets in the other an awkward sense of angularity and rhythmic imprecision arises. As mentioned earlier, triplets can usually become smoother and easier if students practise singing them to the words 'straw-ber-ry' or 'mer-ri-ly' as they play. At the earliest stages, 'Co-ca-Co-la' is helpful when dealing with four successive semiquavers, and of course syllables such as those used in Kodály teaching can be invaluable with all kinds of rhythms (e.g. 'tie-fee' for dotted quavers followed by semiquavers).

Words and structure

With regard to structural unity, appropriately chosen words can have a pivotal role. This is evident in the first movement of Beethoven's 'Les Adieux' Sonata, Op.81a:

The score includes the word 'Lebewohl' (farewell) and splits it into three syllables (Le-be-wohl) over the opening three notes of the sonata. Nothing could be more powerful than these three simple syllables in projecting both the musical shape of the opening falling phrase of the work, as well as the overriding feeling of melancholy and loneliness that will permeate not only the Adagio introduction but also the movement's main Allegro section. This is where Beethoven's three syllables become especially important, as the opening three-note 'Le-be-wohl' sigh motif appears everywhere. If the performer does not practise singing and saying these syllables out loud each time they appear, it will be challenging for the true character of the movement as a whole to emerge. In other words, Beethoven's opening syllables are far from a mere novelty: they are essential to the interpretive raison d'être and whole structural unity of the movement.

Fugues

Singing words out loud on each subject entry whilst practising a fugue is also extremely helpful. Fugue subjects from Bach's *The Well-Tempered Clavier* were given hilarious treatment in this respect by the much-respected Victorian theorist and composer Ebenezer Prout.[25] Here are the words Prout set for the G minor Fugue in Book 1 of *The Well-Tempered Clavier*:

And here is the Prout treatment for the C major Fugue in Book 2:

Whilst this is extremely amusing and useful for relaxing students, during performance it can be helpful to silently sing fugue subjects to chosen words – especially if there is a need for greater concentration and focus when a pianist is feeling nervous. But the big point is that the use of words goes much further than merely providing some relaxation and a means of focus. It provides one of the main ways in which a whole fugue can be shaped and interpreted. Whilst dealing with the often stressful business of sorting out fugal interpretation, the words give a clear sense of the subject's shape and should therefore be applied and indeed sung out loud in practice on every one of the subject's entries.

Breathe like a wind player!

Wind players, like singers, are continuously aware of the need to gauge precisely when to take a breath without interrupting phrasing. Because we do not use our lungs to create a sound on the piano, paradoxically this can make it harder to give the impression of spaciousness, musical clarity and characterful phrasing. As mentioned on p.27, it is tempting for pianists to hold their breath throughout difficult technical passages, thereby making them doubly hard to execute. The good news is that pianists of all levels and abilities can quickly learn breathing techniques that make piano playing much easier to control.

Just as we can learn from string bowing, so we can also benefit from observing how wind instrumentalists control their breathing. It is fascinating to discover where wind players breathe in performance. Woodwind and brass players need to inhale in such a way that the phrasing is not distorted or upset.

---

25 Ebenezer Prout (1835–1909) wrote seminal text books on counterpoint and fugue. His words for all of 'the 48' can be seen in their entirety at http://jessicamusic.blogspot.co.uk/2012/09/ebenezer-prout-not-invented-by-dickens.html.

Breath markers

Once you have got used to the vocalisation practice techniques described earlier, try to sing your entire repertoire out loud as part of your regular practice. Find and mark in all your scores places where it is natural and convenient to breathe. 'Breath markers' are important structural signposts in music. They help to shape, stabilise and clarify interpretations, and generally make playing much easier. Often they tally precisely with simple four-bar periodic phrasing, as in the 'Soldier's March' from Schumann's *Album for the Young*:

When you return to playing – as opposed to singing – your pieces, make a conscious effort to literally inhale and/or exhale at all the breath-marker points on your scores. In the initial stages of understanding how music breathes, it is worth practising overtly melodic pieces of music. At first, you will be dealing with simple exhaling breaths over phrases, with quick inhales to keep you going. But it is also important to learn how to inhale as you rise towards climaxes in phrases. Firstly, imagine the particular orchestral instrument that a phrase could be played on, and then literally breathe as though producing the notes through your mouth rather than through your fingers! In the following example ('First Loss', also from Schumann's *Album for the Young*), imagine that your right hand is a flautist. Inhale and exhale only at the commas marked above the notes:

The use of natural, 'musical' breathing goes hand in hand with a healthy piano technique. Healthy breathing is also the gateway towards sensitive, intelligent and convincing phrasing and structural awareness.

A good example of this from the symphonic concert repertoire is the second subject of Rachmaninov's Piano Concerto No.2, first movement, where the music's melodic ascent can be matched with an expansion of the performer's lungs.

As the phrase falls, it is only natural that the performer will feel the expressive (and physical) need to exhale. This is a classic example of physical and expressive unity in playing. If it is also accompanied by a subtle *accelerando* followed by a *ritardando*, we can then add logical *rubato* (sometimes referred to as 'agogics')[26] into the picture.

At grade 7–8 level, much can be learnt from Grieg's ever-popular 'Notturno' from the *Lyric Pieces* Book 5. This exquisite character piece contains moments that could emulate the midnight call of a nightingale. Here it is desirable to inhale slowly, giving an added depth and expansive breadth to the poetic wistfulness of the phrases as they gradually melt into trills inspired by birdsong (bars 15–17):

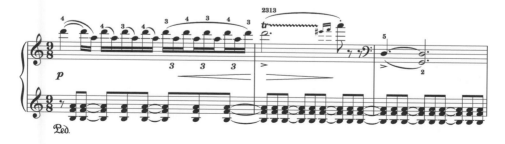

26 A more detailed consideration of agogics appears in Chapter 8.

Finally, an impressionist masterpiece: Debussy's sensuous 'Les sons et les parfums tournent dans l'air du soir', the fourth Prelude from Book 1, provides a classic example of how 'phrase-sensitive' breathing can enhance interpretation, leading to playing that is at once natural and sensuously charged. Subtle virtuosity in breath control is required here to help emphasise the mercurial changes of light and shade:

Bars 1–4

7 Basics of phrasing and structure

Structure

It is vital for performers to understand how the music they play is constructed. Without strong awareness of form and balance, a performance will inevitably meander and lack conviction. This should not surprise us, as virtually all western classical music can be viewed as either a 'journey in sound' or as 'sonic architecture'. But what is surprising is how often even virtuoso pianists can fail to project the logical dimensions in a great masterpiece effectively to an audience. Why is this the case?

To understand structure is to understand how to phrase. Phrasing – the art of making music intelligible, the joy of turning hundreds of notes on the printed page into musical sentences, paragraphs and stories – brings cohesion and logic to musical ideas. Working in partnership with rhythmic discipline, skilful phrasing is the main means by which pianists can bring a clear presentation of the musical flow, line and development to the listener. Think of commas, semicolons, full stops, paragraphs and chapters in a novel and you have a direct literary parallel with logical phrasing in music. Music is a kinetic art, and any performance that does not have logic and shape simply fails to convince.

Rudiments of phrasing

Of course, the basic and most simple phrases in music last for four bars and can most commonly be heard in nursery rhymes. Four-bar 'question' phrases usually open up a new musical idea and frequently finish on the dominant. They are usually followed by a further four-bar 'answer' phrase that neatly concludes on the tonic note of the piece. The resulting eight-bar musical sentence is the basis from which all phrasing in western music from the eighteenth century onwards can be considered. Deviations, modifications and extensions from this norm need to be understood. Players need to be able to show these constructions as they play, just as an orator will need to breathe and take stock temporarily at the ends of sentences, and even after commas. Of course, there are a vast number of rules and regulations that we must all grasp within musical sentences in order to play with authority. These take years of cultivation and assimilation. Traditionally, students gradually assimilate authority and understanding in phrasing through trial and error, picking up guidelines, suggestions, and even gimmicks and 'tricks' almost by default. Mastering the art of shaping music comes after many hours of piano lessons, experience as a listener and a gradual improvement in the art of self-listening.

However, there is a more systematic, methodical alternative. I am indebted to the pianist Carlo Grante for introducing me to two seminal textbooks from the nineteenth century that are in effect exhaustively detailed courses in phrasing, musical inflexions and grammar: *The Principles of Expression in Pianoforte Playing*, by Adolph F. Christiani (Theodore Presser, 1885); and *Musical Expression*, by M. Mathis Lussy (Novello, 1896). Christiani's monumental textbook runs to over 300 pages and begins with a detailed consideration of 'The Motors of Musical Expression' before analysing accentuation, rhythm and metre, metrical and harmonic accents, and dynamics. It concludes with an extensive section on time, including *rubato* and *accelerando*. Lussy's *Musical Expression* includes chapters on metrical, rhythmic and expressive accentuation and is also monumental in scope, running to well over 200 pages. As far as I am aware, these rare textbooks are unique. Fortunately, at the time of writing they are both available on the internet in English translations.[27]

Waves and peaks

Rachmaninov famously said that every piece has one climax. It follows that it is up to the performer to find this point in every work he or she plays, and then fit subsidiary climaxes around the music's central peak. If one keeps on looking for smaller and smaller peaks, and thinks about music as a series of 'waves' rather than points, a logical conviction that is similar to sensitive phrasing will begin to emerge. We can learn a lot from the popular assertion that music is simply a journey towards and away from pivotal notes. Practice here is similar to focusing and refocusing with a pair of binoculars on a landscape in the distance. In many cases, you can experiment as you practise so that the climax is the loudest moment, with other phrase-peaks less loud. Focus on one area at a time, and then go for a broad overview. The opening twelve bars of Erik Satie's first *Gymnopédie* is a good example of hierarchy in phrasing in a musical paragraph:

This piece neatly divides into three four-bar phrases, each of which moves towards the third bar. Experiment in practice by moving towards a mini climax on the first beat of every third bar (performances can be more subtle than this

27 *The Principles of Expression in Pianoforte Playing*: http://d.pr/UBE5; *Musical Expression*: http://d.pr/jOAZ.

and move towards the third or second beats of these bars, but for the moment keep things simple). In this excerpt there are three four-bar phrases. Work at each of these independently, avoiding accents on the second and third beats but moving with a *crescendo* to each climax; then add a *diminuendo* as you move away from them. Look particularly at bars 9–12, the biggest phrase. Find the range of sound you wish for this phrase and then return to the opening so that bars 1–4 are the quietest, with bars 5–8 a little more open in sound, leading to bars 9–12.

Exercises for developing awareness of phrasing

One of the lesser-known facts about the outstanding Scottish Impressionist composer J.B. McEwen (principal of the Royal Academy of Music in London in the 1930s and 40s) is that he wrote a fascinating workbook on the art of phrasing for pianists. As far as I am aware, *Exercises on Phrasing in Pianoforte Playing* (Ricordi, 1908), which McEwen wrote in the early part of his career, remains the only substantial course of exercises written in the UK to develop technical facility in phrasing. Sadly, it is virtually impossible to get hold of, as it has long been out of print. However, the spirit of the book is easy to emulate. Unlike the textbooks by Lussy and Christiani mentioned earlier, the McEwen book contains hardly any words at all. It consists mainly of 100 musical excerpts from all periods – but with all the phrasing, articulation and dynamic markings removed. Students can add their own phrasing to each excerpt, and discuss their efforts with their teachers. They should then 'practise' their attempts at phrasing at the piano and compare what they have 'composed' with what the composers actually wrote. The exercise concludes with the student practising both the composer's phrasing and their own. Short of spending a considerable amount of time working through Lussy and Christiani, I can think of no better way to grasp the fundamentals and learn the technique of phrasing than to experiment with the McEwen approach. Consider knowledge about phrasing as a technical tool for use in interpretation. Used in collaboration with a sympathetic teacher, McEwen's exercises will strengthen your understanding of how music can be shaped, provided that musical instincts, as well as sensitivity and sympathy to the style of each excerpt, are always at the forefront. It can be all too easy to approach the subject of phrasing as one would a crossword puzzle. But never forget that basic musical impulses – singing and dancing – lie at the heart of almost all phrases. It would be folly to forget this when working on the shape, direction and flexibility of any melodic line.

Phrasing in practice

Here are three examples from McEwen's *Exercises on Phrasing in Pianoforte Playing*, reproduced exactly as they appear in the book (that is, with no phrase and articulation markings). I challenge readers to play each one with convincing phrasing!

1 First, some Chopin from the standard concert repertoire. The central section of the first Scherzo in B minor, Op.20, is particularly demanding, as the beautiful melody, originally a Polish Christmas carol, involves repeated notes:

You need to avoid bumps and accents on these. Try to create the impression that all the note repetitions float out of the keyboard. This requires skilful ear–hand coordination and the ability to depress the repeated notes with a shallower touch (the bebung approach from Chapter 4 could prove extremely useful). The texture in this exquisite passage also demands *legatissimo*, skilful pedalling and stretches of up to an eleventh. But by focusing on the direction and shape of the right-hand thumb melody and giving more tonal weight to it, the difficulties in pedalling and balancing become less onerous. The real challenge for the player lies in managing to sustain the melodic line so that there is a sense of momentum, not only with the first G sharp in bar 4 of the excerpt, but also onwards, so that a beautiful eight-bar period unfolds.

2 Schumann's 'Träumerei' from his *Kinderszenen* is one of the most famous melodies in the repertoire:

Though this ever popular miniature can be tackled by pianists from grade 5 level upwards, it requires sensitivity and care in terms of tonal balance and shape. The phrasing challenge largely revolves around the fact that the long notes can break the melodic line all too easily. With the piano, it is especially easy to put an enormous accent after a long note, simply because sound decays extremely quickly; you need to try to hide this by listening carefully to the very end of each long note, then dovetailing effortlessly by playing the short notes that follow at a quieter dynamic level than the final decay of the long note they succeed.

3   Finally, at advanced, diploma level, we have Chopin's C sharp minor Étude, Op.25 No.7, which is particularly demanding from a textural/contrapuntal perspective:

The initial bass ('cello') melody is immediately answered by a treble ('violin') entry in the second bar, while the middle ground ('piano accompaniment') creates the illusion of a still lake. It is very hard to listen carefully to three musical elements simultaneously, and we will not discuss the contrapuntal challenges involved here as this subject comes in Chapter 9. Let's just say that it is advisable to practise each of the three musical strands in this excerpt separately. Dealing with the repeated-quaver middle ground first (the 'piano' part), it is vital that you create a subtle reverberation so that each quaver dovetails effortlessly into the next one. Accents, stiff wrists and too much physical movement are clearly impossible in this context; tepid delicacy, and the ability to kiss the surface of the keys (rather than dig to the bottom of the key bed), are the prerequisites. There are several repeated notes to deal with in the cello and violin melodic lines, and these require sensitive listening in practice. The overall shape of both lines descends with long notes followed by shorter groups, and this can result in lumpy phrasing, as well as a tendency to simply overdo the natural *diminuendo* that many will instinctively feel as they play. In fact, I would argue that the long notes in bars 1, 2 and 3 of the cello part should move naturally towards the highly expressive B sharp of bar 4 of this excerpt. You therefore need to feel a sense of *crescendo* on these long notes, whilst also getting progressively softer on all the short notes in the first four bars. This also needs to be done in the violin part. The challenges that phrasing brings to the surface in this étude are most certainly not for the faint-hearted – good luck!

Structural challenges – rhythmic discipline

An excellent sense of rhythm is essential when you are shaping phrases. Indeed, a unified and logical interpretation that listeners will be able to understand largely depends on rhythmic precision and discipline. This was explained fully in Chapters 2 and 3. If you cannot maintain a regular sense of pulse throughout a performance, the music will become incoherent and distorted. Clarity and focus can be built up by using the metronome as you practise. Be strict and demanding on yourself at all times! Refuse to accept vagueness. It can be useful to record your own playing if you listen back critically. Can you clap or tap a beat as you listen back to your playing? Do you maintain a steady pulse or gradually get faster and faster? If you continue to have problems holding a steady tempo it can help to set the metronome going, sing the melodic part of the problematic piece in question, and move around your piano in a pseudo dance or march-like manner! The importance of singing and movement has of course been stressed at length earlier. In particular, there is nothing quite like dancing for clarifying and stabilising a sense of pulse! In terms of structural cohesion and awareness of what you are doing in a performance, it is good to take an objective bird's-eye view at regular intervals: record yourself, then listen back and try to conduct your performance. If this is easy to do, then your performance has a sense of logical continuity and structural integrity.

If you find one passage challenging in a piece and have to slow down in order to play it, then your overall tempo is too fast. Take your speed for the whole piece from the 'difficult place', even if this speed seems too slow for the opening. It is simply not on to dramatically lose tempo when the going gets tough!

At an intermediate level, tempo connections commonly become controversial when dealing with minuet and trios. Should we keep the same speed going in the trio as adopted in the minuet? Personally, I do not mind if trios change pulse – provided there is immediate conviction and confidence from the performer at the start of each section. Start at a tempo and stick to it. Often a more extended pause between minuet and trio (and before the *da capo*) can make a change of tempo sound more convincing.

Be very careful to realise all your rhythms as precisely as possible. Cavalier inconsistencies in approach to repeated rhythms can wreak havoc on the structure of a piece. This can be heard most readily in dotted rhythms, where casual performers may start off with strong control only to lose focus, resulting in dotted-quaver and semiquaver groupings changing into loose triplet patterns. If you want a disciplined performance, consistency in approach is essential.

The following musical excerpts come from three contrasted passages of 'Für Elise' and are all too often played at totally different speeds from one another. When this happens, the overall logic and structure of Beethoven's beloved miniature is destroyed:

Example 1: bars 1–4

Example 2: bars 25–8

Example 3: bars 79–82

In practice sessions, it is essential to use a metronome so that you can maintain the same pulse for all three sections. When you can connect each section and find a convincing and sustainable tempo from the opening bars, your performance will truly have a convincing sense of structure.

Does this imply that whole movements need to be executed at one continuously exact metronome marking in order to have logic? Hardly! There is nothing machine-like about true artistry. Experienced musicians are able to allow a sense of overall rhythmic unity whilst also enjoying expansive expressive flexibility at appropriate moments. This will be explored in greater detail in Chapter 8.

Let's move on to advanced recital repertoire. Busoni's famous transcription of Bach's Chaconne in D minor, BWV 1004, puts the unity of pulse myth firmly to rest. Of course, the strict musical architecture of a passacaglia, ground bass or chaconne seems to imply rigid adherence to a consistent rhythmic beat, yet Busoni's score is full of changes of tempo. This can immediately be seen by comparing the opening (marked 'Andante maestoso') with the bottom of the second page (marked 'Più mosso') – the first of many tempo shifts.

Moving on to Classical repertoire, it is interesting to try setting the metronome in motion whilst listening to a performance of Beethoven or Mozart by a Brendel, Schiff or Solomon. Many will be surprised to see how quickly the pulse can vary, leaving the metronome far behind. The point is that what really matters is a listener's *perception* of unity of pulse. Of course, metronome practice is invaluable for pianists when they are developing a sense of rhythmic discipline, but ultimately the human interpreter's sense of momentum, expectation and release in performance will create a flow that is much more meaningful than the incessant ticking of a machine. However, in music from the twentieth or twenty-first centuries, created during the 'machine age', it is often extremely effective to aim for zero tolerance as far as speed deviation goes. Works such as Prokofiev's Toccata need exceptional control and discipline, so that it would be perfectly possible for a metronome to tick along consistently throughout a single live performance with absolutely no adjustment from machine or interpreter.

Colour and structure

Contrasts of colour and touch can be used to clearly show the form of a piece. This can be demonstrated in virtually every fugue of *The Well-Tempered Clavier*. I recommend contrasts of dynamics as a general rule when playing episodes in fugues: for example, the beautiful, expressive episodes in the D major fugue from Book 1 are totally different from the fanfare-like nature of the fugue's subject, so a quieter dynamic perspective in each episode would appear desirable. And contrasted approaches to dynamics and, perhaps more importantly, articulation can vibrantly 'set off' the differences between subject and counter-subject in many a fugue from *The Well-Tempered Clavier*. I recommend playing the subject of the C minor fugue with a mixture of *staccato* and *legato* throughout, then playing the counter-subject on every recurrence completely *legato*. Such an approach helps to emphasise the form and logic of the piece to the listener. In the great C sharp minor fugue from Book 1 there are three fugue subjects to project, and it makes sense to adopt totally different sounds for each one (a deep tone for the opening, with its long, hushed and expressive semibreves; a lighter touch for the circling sequential quavers that form the second subject; and finally a more assertive, piercingly resonant sound for the third subject's rising fourth and repeated crotchets).

Motivic structural connections

It is important for pianists to be able to follow the composer's own compositional journey in performance by highlighting the changes that melodic fragments undergo throughout a piece. Making oneself aware of alterations, decorations, extensions and contractions to themes in a set of variations, for instance, will lead to exciting interpretive decisions. If a performer can highlight specific pitches in an elaborate variation that relate to notes in the work's opening theme, then the performance will most certainly affect the listener's overall understanding and appreciation.

This is of course a large subject, but readers interested in applying the principles of motivic development and unity to their interpretations should first study the seminal text books on this subject by Arnold Schoenberg and Rudolph Reti.[28]

In variation forms, it is usually excellent structural practice to shape the motifs from opening themes and all subsequent variations in the same way throughout. Often this can lead to interpretive decisions that may not concur with one's immediate instincts. For example, in Schumann's Op.1 – his brilliant 'Abegg' Variations – it is probably best not to shape the opening of the final variation towards the middle of the second full bar. To do so would lead to a 'regular' four-bar period in the opening line, but this would be contrary to the shaping indicated by Schumann in the theme:

---

28   Rudolph Reti Publisher: Macmillan (1951), ISBN 978-0837198750; *Arnold Schoenberg Fundamentals of Composition*, ed. Gerald Strang and Leonard Stein (re-issued Faber 1999).

The opening of Schumann's theme is made up of four two-bar units, with the emphasis in each unit on the final, two-beat note. When Schumann's final variation is thought through in a similar way, a subtle emphasis on the first beats of bars 2 and 4, as well as bars 6 and 8, becomes both logical and necessary (the *diminuendo* in bar 3 means that the emphasis at the beginning of the fourth bar needs to be done by delay and/or a subtle change in colour).

Technical facility and structure

There are many fascinating connections between technical facility and structure, particularly in the virtuoso repertoire. In études which have wall to wall semiquavers in every bar, playing becomes extremely tiring if each note is focused on separately. It is much easier to think of each phrase unit in a virtuoso étude as a single gesture. By coordinating many tiny movements into one large gesture, relaxation and facility become easier. Worthy of mention in connection with this subject are the four Chopin Scherzos, each of which makes use of a four-bar structure for phrasing. In performance it is much easier to breathe in the space between the four-bar phrases, and to try to think of four beats rather than four bars for each phrase. But it is important to work at music from several different perspectives, even in the easiest repertoire. We will look at this in more detail in Chapter 10 ('Speed'). Meanwhile, let's take one of Bach's celebrated G major minuets (BWV 116) from the 'Anna Magdalena' notebook as an example of how this approach can work in the earliest stages:

Begin by practising with an emphasis on every single quaver. Use the metronome at first if that helps, setting it at quaver = 120. Next, concentrate on the crotchets. Set the metronome at crotchet = 60 and feel three accents per bar rather than the six you felt when focusing on quavers. After this, try to feel one whole bar as a beat. Only some metronomes have the capacity to show crotchet = 30, so you will need to feel an enormously expansive gesture in your body that can sweep you forward from one bar to the next. The point is that you are feeling the minuet in dotted minims rather than smaller notes. Finally, it should be possible to feel internally four whole bars in one gigantic musical sweep. I find it useful to move my hands in wave movements as I do this, with one ascending arm movement corresponding to one whole bar. It is also useful to try to inhale for four bars, then exhale for another four. Focusing your proverbial musical binoculars on different perspectives in this manner can have an enormous effect on the way listeners perceive the music's structure. It is also extremely beneficial for building up security and understanding of the music you are recreating.

8 Playing with line and *rubato*

So is phrasing and structure all about proportion and intellectual calculation? All head and little heart? Is the answer simply to get out a coloured pencil and draw circles around the 'peak' notes in every phrase? Well this might be a fair starting point, but after a short time, the exercise would become predictable and pointless – or it should do so! Finding a way to phrase seamlessly, to 'hold the line' and unify the melodic contours of a piece into an organic whole, is clearly of paramount importance in music-making. With advanced students, teachers normally spend a considerable amount of time and energy working towards this essential ideal, as it is only by cultivating convincing phrasing that a pianist can hope to emulate the art of a great singer. But within this unified melodic flow, music needs to breathe and have expansive spaciousness. The art of phrasing is not so much about finding peaks as about discovering the technique to move towards and away from them naturally and with an involved sense of musical commitment. In order to play with soulful passion, it is necessary to sing through the pivots in music, softening the angles and finding the luxurious line, which can connect everything into one glorious and continuous organic whole. This can be achieved through use of the vocalisation and breathing techniques described in Chapter 6. Closely allied to singing is physical movement and dancing in particular. The importance of learning to move and dance internally was mentioned in Chapter 2. Let us apply these principles to a famous piece from the elementary repertoire: the Minuet in G minor BWV115 from the 'Anna Magdalena' notebook:

Practising by swinging from side to side in time to this minuet (or even quite literally dancing around the room as you hum it) will certainly help you to shape your interpretation. You can also try conducting it as you sing through the right hand, noting the way in which the melodic 'waves' move towards and then away from climax notes. If you know where you are going to and from in a piece at all times, then you have solved most of its interpretive issues!

Moving towards organic unity; playing with line

In the most convincing performances of music from all levels of difficulty there is a sense of unity and oneness between the pianist and the piano. Technical and musical discipline fuses into an effortless, organic whole so that phrasing and physical movements from the player seem completely natural, inevitable and authoritative. In great playing there is always a sense of ease and simplicity. In such cases, the pianist's hands seem a natural extension of the keyboard. Technical control merges completely with musical intent.

How does one achieve this level of excellence? What can one do to reach this ultimate height of 'enhanced discipline'? Of course, discipline will only come, if it is going to come, after many years of hard practice, struggle and thought. However, one can certainly begin afresh and immediately improve one's playing by adopting a few essential attributes that can guide the long journey ahead. Technically, the two essential attributes of feeling the rhythmic pulse (like a dancer) and breathing the melodic lines (like a singer) will feel easier if fingers are close to the keys and if the general mechanical approach reduces the 'hit' element in articulation in favour of the 'touch and press' approach. It is also helpful to see phrases and sequences of notes together rather than in isolation, and to enhance this feeling of unity within pieces by emphasising linear rather than vertical movements.

By way of an introduction to this pianistic approach, we can begin by practising five-finger exercises and scales with our eyes closed. Focus on the actual sounds and their afterglow – avoid being distracted. Keep your fingers as close to the keys as possible. Avoid any unnecessary vertical movements as you play. Accentuation tends to separate notes, which is the exact opposite of what we are trying to achieve here. Breathe with your phrasing. Sing through rests. Relax your arms and play with a sense of transfer – make one note glide effortlessly into the next by adopting circular elbow movements as you move from note to note. This can be illustrated with arrows and an undulating line below a scale fragment or a five-finger exercise:[29]

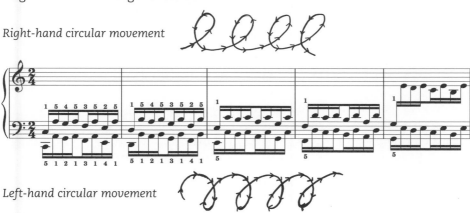

Right-hand circular movement

Left-hand circular movement

Hanon: The Virtuoso Pianist in sixty exercises (1873), No.6

29 Circular elbow movements are illustrated here by the wave-line. The five loops indicate the lowest point for the elbows as they travel in circles in each bar (left elbow in clockwise movement, right in anti-clockwise movement).

After this, it is interesting to move on to Czerny. Amidst the busy passagework, it is important to take control of the pulse and glide elegantly through the dense forest of semiquavers with a sense of horizontal line and purpose. As you develop towards projection and control of the 'inner rhythm' and line, it can be helpful to move in time to the pulse whilst practising. Try moving your entire torso in complete circles as you play the following excerpt from Czerny: *The Art of Finger Dexterity*, Op.740 No.1 (typical of so many in this composer's prolific collection of studies):

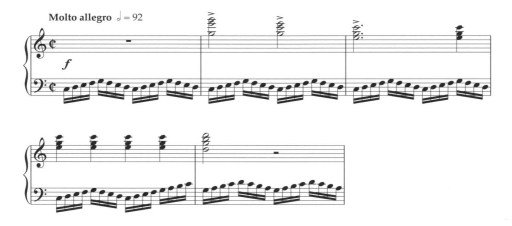

Move around slowly in a clockwise direction, then try the same thing anti-clockwise. Aim to synchronise your circular movements with the music you are playing in such a way that you complete one revolution from start to finish in the time it takes to play one complete bar – no more and no less. The circular movements focus your mind and body on the broad rhythmic flow of the étude, taking your mind away from each individual semiquaver. When you 'let go' and focus on the broad sweep of what you are playing rather than on every single note, you are looking at the forest as a whole rather than at each tree in turn. It almost goes without saying that this broad overview should come into place once each individual section of the study has been practised and thoroughly assimilated.

Rocking from side to side on the piano stool is another means of 'letting go' and allowing a sense of line to take flight. Though the central trio from Schumann's celebrated 'Knight Rupert' in *Album for the Young* (see overleaf) can easily be practised with circular movements, it is beneficial to rock from side to side with it too: lean slowly to your right-hand side for two bars, then reverse the process and lean to the left for the next two bars. I recommend practising this exercise along with slow inhales and exhales: breathe in as you move to the right, and breathe out as you move left:

In playing with line it can help to imagine that the keyboard is curved rather than flat. Thinking in wave patterns, and imagining your hands and wrists rising and falling as they travel horizontally onwards with an undulating line, is a good means of inspiring playing that is accent-free, flowing and 'organic' in the sense that the pianist's body and approach connect effortlessly to the piano. Playing with line helps to blur the separation between piano and pianist to the extent that they become one and the same thing.

Rubato

Rubato, literally 'robbed time', involves a flexibility of speed within a given tempo. Both *accelerandos* and *ritardandos* are involved in the execution of *rubato*, which serves to heighten the expressive powers of interpretation. The literature on *rubato* is extensive, beginning with the preface to Frescobaldi's *Fiori Musicali* (1630). There is no doubt that composers from the Baroque to the present day have expected performers to use it, and it is as prevalent in popular, jazz and folk music as in classical. The term was even used at one point (c.1800) to indicate modifications of dynamics rather than tempo. Some believe that this was what Chopin had in mind when he used the word (see many of the *Mazurkas*, where *rubato* appears to be used to encourage accents on normally weak beats). Here we will examine two types of *rubato*: *rubato* that affects the melody only, not the accompaniment; and *rubato* that concerns every part of the musical make-up.

Melodic *rubato*

In melodic *rubato*, the left hand acts as the proverbial police officer, keeping a strict control of the pulse whilst the right hand meanders. It always needs to get back under control, in synchronisation with the left. Perhaps the best way of immediately understanding what this means is to hear a jazz combo in performance, with the bass and drum players fixing the structure via repetition whilst the sax player improvises around them. In Baroque music, the florid variations in a passacaglia or ground bass can be viewed as 'notated *rubato*', and performers in such contexts should feel freedom as they execute fast virtuoso runs between the slower, fixed-note patterns below.

It is easy to see how melodic *rubato* can be applied to Chopin's *Berceuse*, Op.57, with its continuously repeated left-hand rhythmic ostinato:

In this piece, the right hand weaves exquisite, quasi-improvisatory filigree passagework between the left-hand quaver figuration. The scope for adjusting pacing, shading and tonal colours in the right-hand part is infinite, and at the highest level of interpretation it should be spontaneous. Within the fixed discipline of the controlled rhythm in the bass, freedom is limitless. This type of rhythmic flexibility is sometimes referred to as 'Chopin *rubato*', in which the left hand maintains a strict pulse and the right hand is 'free' above – but within the left hand's strict guidelines.

All-encompassing *rubato*

But Chopin's *Berceuse* need not have its *rubato* restricted exclusively to the right-hand part: if you adopt an 'all in one' approach linking *rubato* to phrase structure, then it is certainly possible to try subtle *rubato* in the left hand too. Many musicians see compositions in terms of waves, with ebbs and flows gently urging the music forwards and then away in a whole series of climaxes, some bigger than others. In this respect 'right-hand only' *rubato* may not be so convincing. An alternative approach, which is perhaps more universal and relevant to all kinds of different stylistic contexts, is 'all-encompassing *rubato*'. This second species is modelled on agogics[30] and is more readily connected to other aspects of interpretation – notably shading, pedalling and structure. These four elements together (pedalling, shading, *rubato* and structure) are used in all-encompassing *rubato* to articulate clearly the peaks and troughs of phrasing. This approach puts all the interpretive eggs in the same proverbial basket! Firstly, decide where the phrase begins, peaks and stops. Let your pedalling work in collaboration with your phrasing: you can gradually use more pedal as you reach the top note of a phrase, then taper off as the phrase unwinds. Dynamics can follow a similar pattern: *crescendo* towards the phrase's climax, then *diminuendo* away from it. In terms of *rubato* it makes sense to gradually increase speed to the peak of the phrase, enjoy the top note by projecting a sense of arrival on it, then gradually slow down towards the phrase's ending.

30 H. Reimann first used this term in 1884 to describe interpretive subtleties achieved through modifications of tempo, including *rallentandos* and *accelerandos*, as well as dwelling on notes, breathing sounds, rests, fermatas and *rubato*.

Figures of eight

All-encompassing *rubato* needs to sound natural and effortless in order to be convincing. In order to master the technique of using *rubato* in this way, imagine you are a conductor. Begin by practising drawing figures of eight in the air whilst singing out loud eight-bar phrases:

Figures of eight   *Figures of eight*

Practise synchronising different parts of the figure of eight you are drawing in the air with different parts of the melody you are singing. The start and finish of the figure of eight should coincide with an accented note. Let's begin practising this with the celebrated second subject from the first movement of Chopin's Piano Concerto No.1 in E minor, Op.11. Firstly, try to make the lowest parts of the figure of eight you are drawing in the air coincide with the first beats of each bar you are singing:

Next, try a slower movement in your arm as you draw the figures of eight and aim to make the lowest parts of it coincide with the first notes in every other bar:

Finally, try an extremely slow arm movement for your airborne figure of eights so that the lowest part of each figure coincides with the first beat in every fourth bar:

Having mastered the technical skill of singing whilst drawing figure of eights in the air, it makes sense to practise playing the Chopin melody on the piano with your right hand whilst continuing to draw figure-of-eight movements in the air with your left. Once this is mastered, you can attempt to sing and then play the right-hand part on its own with *accelerando* and *ritardandos* whilst drawing the movements in the air with your left hand. If this is working properly, you will find that you elongate the side of the figures you are drawing in the air as you slow down. As you speed up, you will find that the sides of the figures compress. Imagine a conductor with large arm movements for slow expansive phrases, and smaller, compact movements for faster phrases. This is a crucial step in learning how to produce convincingly authoritative and natural all-encompassing *rubato*. Natural ease and fluency may take time to acquire, so it is important to practise both hands separately. The left hand of the Chopin example above should be practised on its own whilst the right hand draws figures of eight up in the air. In practice sessions, try to coordinate pedal, shading and *rubato* so that there is a feeling of *accelerando* and *crescendo* in the natural move towards the beginning of the third bar as the climax of the phrase.

Moving to the fifth bar in eight-bar sentences

The repertoire is full of eight-bar constructions in which the fifth bar is a mini-climax that needs recognition. An effective way of showing phrasing expressively but naturally is to use all-encompassing *rubato*, keeping the figure-of-eight movements firmly in your inner ear as you accelerate then *ritardando* away from the middle of the musical sentence. This can clearly be seen in Chopin's E flat minor Étude, Op.10 No.6:

There are literally dozens of similar examples of this in Chopin's oeuvre and elsewhere. In many instances it is good to begin eight-bar phrases slowly, then gradually and naturally *crescendo* and accelerate towards fifth-bar peaks. After this, a *diminuendo* and *ritardando* towards the end of the eighth bar completes the picture. The result will be more natural and convincing if it is possible for a conductor to follow your *rubato*, and a singer to imitate your melodic contour. Therefore, it is good to regularly and consistently practise conducting your own *rubato* using the figure-of-eight technique above with your left hand whilst playing the melody with your right. In this way, you can immediately sense whether or not your phrasing has a smooth, inevitable flow – or an awkward angular sense. If you can follow this up by singing your melody line whilst conducting an *accelerando* and *ritardando* away from the piano, you will begin to gradually build an inner awareness of what constitutes natural phrasing.

Random *rubato*

The extent to which *rubato* is used depends on the stylistic and musical context and the preference of the performer. If the principles are understood, it is inspirational to leave precise execution to chance, mood and whim. The acid test of whether *rubato* convinces or not relates directly to whether or not it is possible to move, sing and breathe along with it. A performer's ability to 'hold on' to the melodic line, to sustain a phrase, to expand via never-ending richness of tone and connection between phrases can make heavy and wayward use of *rubato* possible. If a listener can conduct a performance that uses *rubato* without feeling that their conducting loses smoothness and natural ease, then the *rubato* adopted has integrity. Let's now consider a possible technique for the development of 'impulsive' *rubato*.

The technical development of rhythmic spontaneity

As mentioned earlier, music needs to breathe. Metronomes cannot hope to reproduce the natural ease with which a convincing performer shapes phrases. Bringing emotion and feeling to playing via random, spur-of-the-moment *rubato* is a sign of artistry. Sadly, there seems to be a widely circulated opinion that it is impossible to teach this. It is as though a performer's ability to linger expressively on particular notes for split seconds at a time is entirely down to talent and genius. I do not believe this to be the case, though certainly it is easy to detect artificial attempts at sensitivity whereby performers seem to wait on selected beats or notes in an attempt to show 'significance' or pathos. Music is a kinetic art, and if you interfere with its natural, organic flow, then you risk distortion and a loss of natural ease. On the other hand, there are ways of encouraging variety and improvisatory expression within the rules of music.

'Lingering' techniques

It is indeed possible to practise lingering on notes within the context of a natural rhythmic flow. Let's return to elementary repertoire. Here is an interesting exercise that can be used to manufacture spontaneity in practice. Let's go back to the 'figure of eight' technical principle as described under 'all-encompassing *rubato*', above. Using your left hand for the figures of eight, synchronise your movements in time to the right hand as it plays the melody line in Schumann's 'First Loss' from *Album for the Young*:

If you can keep an ebb and flow going as you play, then it is possible within that broad figure-of-eight arm movement to linger on selected melody notes in turn. Try playing the phrase firstly sitting on the G (first note) then play it again but move to the F sharp (second note) and give it a *tenuto*. Continue and experiment with *tenutos* on all six notes of the opening phrase. If you can keep your left hand conducting smoothly in the air as you play, it is possible to make all six versions of the right-hand line convincing. This approach works extremely well when you want to bring rhythmic variety to music that contains a lot of repeated passages. Quite often it is extremely dull simply to play each repeated phrase in exactly the same way. Let's move on to diploma-level repertoire. In the main theme of Liszt's celebrated concert Étude No.3, 'Un Sospiro' it is possible to keep a feeling of movement going with the swirling arpeggios (via a figure-of-eight approach) whilst leaning on the various repetitions of the motif on different notes:

Try leaning on the first melody note (A flat), then move forward; try using the second note (B flat) as the tenuto pitch. Move towards it, sit on it, and then move forward again! Continue and experiment by holding on to each of the eight notes in the motif in turn, using them all individually as 'peak' notes. You therefore have eight possible versions – eight interpretive choices – to call upon. It is entirely up to you which one you choose, but it makes sense to vary the way you shape this motif on each of its repetitions or transposed presentations in the piece.

How many pianists take time to experiment through shaping phrases in all the different ways possible? Hours and hours can profitably be spent searching for the sounds. It does not matter how easy or advanced the repertoire is – the technical principle remains the same. As in music, so in words too. Think about all the different ways in which you can change a sentence's tone and even meaning simply by leaning a little longer on different words. Memorably, Dame Fanny Waterman showed this in her book *On Piano Teaching and Performing* (Faber Music, 2006) through Shakespeare's famous lines, 'To be or not to be, that is the question'. You can extract ten different meanings from this single line by elongating each of its ten words in turn.

Rubato as a sign of love

It is important that when we play, we should try to love what we are playing. We need time to show what we love. Pianists can see themselves as the musical equivalent of enthusiastic guides at a National Trust castle, taking time and effort to share special things with visitors on a guided tour! Take time to 'gloat' on an expressive appoggiatura or other ornament. Lean and project sensitivity by extending an expressive falling interval. Voice a dominant-seventh chord lovingly, with extra weight and depth of tone on the particular inner note that makes the chord special. If we can show significant features in the music we play, we are sharing with the listener things that we feel. Harnessing this to a natural, flowing rhythmic ebb and flow will prevent performances from ever becoming wayward, artificial or self-indulgent. Let's take three examples from the concert repertoire to show this.

Further examples of *rubato*

The first four bars of the slow movement in Haydn's C minor Sonata (Hob. XVI/20, 'Andante con moto') sound metronomic and wooden without a little *rubato* from the pianist:

Here *rubato* helps to lift the repetitive right-hand crotchets off the page and into the 'con moto' mood stipulated. By conducting and singing away from the piano it is possible to find a natural, almost imperceptible, *accelerando* towards the pivotal G–F appoggiatura at the beginning of bar 3. It is also beneficial to execute the trill in the second bar with an *accelerando*. To play it absolutely evenly is to risk prosaic dullness.

Chopin's beloved G minor Ballade, Op.23, highlights the need to dovetail from section to section via the use of discreet *rubato* in order to unify a performance. The horn motif in the left hand, which leads into the famous theme at bar 68, slows down the tempo:

Clearly, bar 68 needs to begin in exactly the same tempo as bar 67. The pianist is required to smoothly and naturally lilt forward, wave-like, towards and beyond the series of 'mini peaks' that occur in bars 70, 72 and beyond. If the high point here is bar 72 (bar 7 of the excerpt), then the whole section needs to be handled so that a conductor could easily move with an *accelerando* towards that point before gently ebbing away from it. Nothing can be angular, forced or unnatural if conviction is the goal.

Finally, the opening of Fauré's Nocturne No.6 in D flat, Op.63 presents a more subtle *rubato* challenge because of its crucially significant upbeat:

Melodically, the emphasis would appear to centre in this passage on the held, descending triadic notes in the upper part (D flat, A flat and F followed by A flat, F and E flat, etc.). Emphasis in this way would lead to a large *ritardando* engulfing the four-bar phrase, as the descending pattern implies a fusion of *diminuendo* with a slackening of tempo. But emphasis on first beats and a lightening of all upbeats leads to phrasing that has an upward surge (F–G natural–A flat) in the held upper melody line from the beginning of the first full bar), so that *rubato* can actually work when one does the opposite! Emphasis on first beats thus leads to a subtle *accelerando* combined with a *crescendo* towards G flat at the beginning of the second bar. A *rallentando* can then round off this intriguing four-bar segment naturally, setting up *rubato* convincingly for the remainder of the piece.

Shaping phrases with unity, line and *rubato* depends on an acute awareness and projection of rhythm; and music needs to breathe naturally in order to communicate with the listener. Awareness of the techniques required to achieve these goals is more than half of the battle towards success. Confidence will undoubtedly develop with sufficient reflection, patience, determination and regular practice.

9 Sounds: vertical development

Balance and texture

Even the most simple of piano pieces can present challenging issues with regard to balancing the hands. Much of the repertoire we play requires a strong melodic line to be projected over less important figuration – we need to be a 'soloist' in one hand and an 'accompanist' in the other. The fact that the accompaniment part is usually written in the lower part of the piano does not help matters, as the bass strings are bigger and more naturally resonant than those in the treble register of the instrument – where the melody is commonly situated. Fortunately, there are some simple exercises and approaches that are worth practising and developing from the earliest stages in order to become skilful at managing texture. Let's look at some of these briefly.

The piano lid

Practising your pieces on the lid of the piano can be very revealing. Try to make lots of finger noise with the melody hand and as little noise as possible with the hand playing the accompaniment part. This is fun to do and quickly yields results if practised for a few minutes of work each day. You can follow on from this by working at scales with different dynamic levels in each hand. Exaggerate as much as possible so that there is no doubt over which hand is louder than the other! *Fortissimo* in the right hand with *pianissimo* in the left in one play through should be followed by a quick role reversal so that you then try to play as loudly as possible in the left hand whilst the right plays as softly as you can. Continue this approach by varying articulation between the hands. *Staccatissimo* in the left hand with ultra-smooth *legato* in the right makes for an excellent exercise, particularly if it is immediately followed by an exact hand reversal, and then developed by utilising contrasted dynamics in each hand as well.

You should also work at your pieces with lots of exaggerated arm movement in the melody hand whilst keeping the accompaniment hand as quiet and still as possible. Extend your horizons further by playing the melody part conventionally whilst 'playing' the accompaniment part on your knee, or on the music stand above the keyboard. You can also reverse this process in order to develop coordination and highlight the difference between the hands in an additional way.

Managing to project different gradations of sound simultaneously with control and conviction takes time and experience. In the opening of Chopin's famous Prelude in B minor, Op.28 No.6, it is essential for the beautiful, cello-inspired left-hand melody to soar with sonority and richness over the much lighter, wistful and mournful right-hand triads that accompany it above:

Though this miniature masterpiece can be tackled by pianists from grade 4 upwards, its challenges in terms of tonal balancing are daunting even for advanced players. However, a good start can be made if you aim for a completely different technical approach in each hand. Prepare each right-hand triad in advance by touching the keys before you play them. Articulate each chord by 'lifting' every one out of the piano, drawing your fingers towards your body whilst adopting a relaxed wrist movement to prevent stiffness, bumps and notes that do not speak. In total contrast, the left hand needs an impressive depth of tone. In order to develop sonorous sonic power, exaggeration can certainly help. Work in the early stages by moving downwards into the keys on each note at a 45° angle. It should feel as though you are depressing every key as far as it can go. Obviously, you will need to bring refinement and subtlety to your balancing in order to develop the requisite stylistic sensitivity, but in the first stages it will help if you try to imagine you are literally pushing the piano forwards with each finger in turn. Of course, in the standard nineteenth-century repertoire this approach is more often seen in reverse, as most pieces have the main melodic interest in the right hand and the accompaniment part in the left. Paderewski's vintage recording of the Chopin F sharp minor Nocturne, Op.15 No.2, mentioned earlier (p.67), stands as a shining example of how to project right-hand melody with golden tone over an accompaniment. Paderewski was a master in the art of textural control and voicing. An analysis of what he did shows that in passages marked '*piano*' in the score, the melodic line is often played *forte*, whilst the bass and lower treble-clef accompaniment textures remain *pianissimo*.

Texture, voicings and colour counterpoint

It is fascinating and invaluable to experiment by prioritising different voicings in the same passage. Try this out with the simplest of four-part hymns or Bach chorales. Schumann's chorale from his *Album for the Young* is excellent for beginning to work on voicing and can be tackled even by the youngest and most inexperienced of players:

At the other end of the spectrum from Schumann's Chorale in terms of technical difficulty comes Rachmaninov's second piano concerto, Op.18 (see p.19). Its opening is one of the most celebrated phrases for testing the bass register of instruments. The excerpt can be isolated and used as an exercise to build up contrapuntal clarity and awareness. Try repeating this line up to seven times, bringing out different strands of the texture in turn: first try the top notes *ff* and everything else *pp*; then bring out the second highest note in each chord *ff* with the rest *pp*, and so on until the lowest bass notes of each chord are emphasised the most. If you can make this passage sound totally different on each repetition, then you are well on the way to cultivating a technique that will really project inner voices and counterpoint clearly in a public venue.

Towards a polyphonic technique: separating sounds in one hand

But how exactly does all of this work in practice? Contrapuntal clarity and voicing within a single hand does not simply come from having good ears and excellent intentions! Learning to separate one melodic strand from another using the same hand is a specific technical skill that can be acquired. It takes time, patience and perseverance. Are there any weaknesses in your fingers when you play three or four notes at the same time in one hand? Here is an exercise for all levels of pianists to test and develop your chordal playing: begin by playing four-note chords at *mezzo forte* level with arm weight and the 'touch and press' approach. Repeat each chord four times, but after each repetition leave each one of the notes from the chord ringing on in turn. The held note should sound strong and assured in each case:

If this proves difficult, try preparing each chord in advance by arpeggiation:

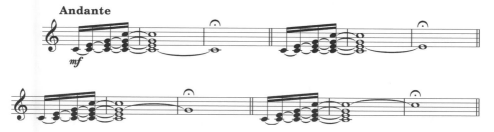

You can do this for chordal passages in repertoire to check notes as well as coordination.

Return to playing a four-note chord with repetitions. On each repetition focus mentally on a different note in the chord. Imagine an infrared laser light beaming down from your shoulders through your arm, wrist and fingertip until it powers through the keybed of the note you are focusing on, working its way down to the wood of the keyboard itself:

After this exercise has been mastered, practise splitting your hand into two contrasted units and working at simple two-part exercises with one voice *forte* and *legato* and the other *piano* and *staccato*. Imagine the laser beam zoning in on the *forte*, *legato* part. Make it weighted and heavy. Dig into the keys, bedding them down to the wood. By way of total contrast, keep the other part as light as possible, concentrating on upward movements and release:

After coping with mixed articulation in one hand, try playing both voices *legato* in phrases for both hands separately, holding them down and utilising 'touch and press' technique. It is important to keep the wrist and lower arm in alignment with each other at the precise moment that each note sounds.[31] Always ensure that one part has more weight and projection than the other. If you can remain relaxed and coordinated, and keep a firm mental picture of the laser beam empowering the stronger part as you play, it should be possible to project a convincing dynamic difference between the two voices.

Two-part technique should be developed to the extent that you can easily play phrases in one hand with equal dynamics, or with either the top part or the lower part significantly louder. You should practise two-part passages so that they can be played *legato* in each voice, or with one part *legato* and the other *staccato*. At all times there should be good coordination, with relaxed focus providing the means to achieve an even and consistent tone in both parts. There should be no 'blank' notes which fail to speak when depressed. The excellent exercises in Chapter 4 of Alfred Cortot's *Rational Principles of Piano Technique* provide further development for polyphonic technique.

Pianists at all levels can enjoy developing warm-up routines by simply playing through chord sequences at the start of each day. More advanced players can move on to experimentation with Bach chorales and hymns. Imagine that each of your fingers is a member of a glorious choir. Allow yourself the opportunity to play Bach's chorale four times, singing out loud each vocal part in turn as you play. This can be extended so that you play only three of the voices but sing the fourth.

After this, try playing the chorale four times again, minus the singing but with an exaggerated emphasis on each voice in turn. Relax and sink into the keys of the highlighted voice, imagining that an infrared beam is warming each note.

---

31   See Chapter 2, 'Alignment', in *The Foundations of Technique*.

Experienced players often use this process when working on a Bach fugue. When cultivated patiently and regularly, it unquestionably sharpens finger independence, aural awareness and general coordination.

It is impossible to overstate the importance of acquiring a strong polyphonic technique. Being able to control more than one voice in the same hand simultaneously is crucial for coordination and control, and many believe that pianists should work systematically through a selection of the Bachian ladder, progressing from a selection of the two-part inversions before moving on to the three-part pieces (sometimes called 'Sinfonias') and then *The Well-Tempered Clavier*, Books 1 and 2 (48 Preludes and Fugues) and 'Art of Fugue'. Indeed, many professional musicians over the generations regularly began their practice sessions each day by playing through some of 'the 48', turning the routine into an almost spiritual daily ritual.

Colour counterpoint

Counterpoint is one of the most significant aspects of pianism, and it should not be limited to works that are primarily fugal or imitative. On the contrary, it is important to view all passages that simultaneously exploit different colours and touches as being contrapuntal. I use the term 'colour counterpoint' to describe many a situation in which the pianist has to utilise different touches virtually at the same time. It is not uncommon to need to project a *cantabile* melody with overlapping *legato* notes above quieter right-hand triadic figurations whilst also playing deep, booming left-hand bass octaves and spinning left-hand arpeggios. The really convincing artist will be able to project each strand of the texture in these instances in such a way that everyone will be aware of the variety of sound. But to do so requires awareness of what is being produced and of what is being heard. Control of tempo, articulation – and even gesture – will all enhance the projection of colour counterpoint and changes of dynamics.

Projecting colour counterpoint

Most pianistic discussions of colour end up with a detailed examination of the French impressionistic repertoire. Let's cut to the chase and move immediately to Debussy's masterful suite *Estampes*. The three music examples below come from 'Pagodes' (the first movement of *Estampes*). The first three bars provide an archetypical instance of 'colour counterpoint', requiring four different touches from the performer:

1   Practise the low fifths of the first beats in bars 1 and 3. They may be distant, but they require strength and resonance in order for the primeval exoticism of distant bells to be evoked convincingly. Use of the back muscles, preparation of the fingers on the key surface prior to execution, and more weight on the B natural rather than the F sharp will all help to realise this.

2   Next, practise the second beats of bars 1 and 2. Here I prefer to project the F sharp rather than the B natural, and the richer, more direct sonority that results envelops the whole sound spectrum that is the opening section of the piece, especially if the fifth is realised with an undulating and relaxed arm movement that allows the sound to glow and resonate after the keys are depressed.

3   Move on to the major-second interval (the F sharp and G sharp in the third/fourth beats of bar 1) taken by the left hand crossing over the right: by lifting the hand off after playing the interval and allowing the sound to float on into the next bar, a quasi-mystical glow creates an alluring and exotic impression that sets the tone for the whole piece. It is important to balance this interval with sensitivity, and I enjoy giving priority to the high G sharp – a truly magical colour within the veiled *pianissimo* backcloth of the texture.

4   Lastly in this excerpt, look at the melody in the top part of bar 3. If you over-project it you risk ruining the subtle evocation of Debussy's rarified art. To under-play it is to lose presence and conviction, turning the music into an apology rather than an exotic reverie. I prefer to only half depress the keys in this particular melodic line – this allows the music to glow and gently sparkle. To depress them any further than this could immediately ruin the interpretation, bringing heaviness, even triteness, into the picture.

Let's move on a little further in 'Pagodes', to bar 41. This is a monumental and climactic moment. The 'out of doors' aesthetic prevalent in the whole piece is enhanced by taking the arresting six-note chords presented here with full body weight – whilst making sure that each chord is lifted away from the keyboard:

Provided their hands are not too small, pianists of all levels can practise chords from this bar in isolation. Nothing could be more wrong than an approach that emphasises physical *legato* by attempting to overlap the chords through staying close to the keyboard. The low C sharp should be taken 'con pugno' (literally 'with your left-hand fist'!) and allowed maximum percussive glow – this is music deeply indebted to the Javanese gamelan, and it is probably too mild and meek to use a solitary finger at this point for a sonority designed to inspire.

The final excerpt from 'Pagodes' (bars 97–8) requires exceptional control from the pianist:

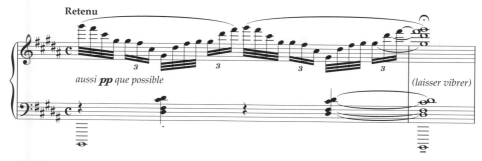

The filigree right-hand figurations evoke a tropical haze, an oriental vision in which sunset is mixed in a background of distant but never indistinct sounds. Obviously, these will not come from conventional work on rhythms, nor from a conventional approach to articulation. I try to depress the keys at the shallowest level and execute the arpeggio groupings with a scratching movement of each finger, flicking each finger in turn, domino-like, towards my body. Meanwhile, in the left hand it is necessary to have coordination and control of arm weight and body weight: the low B (first beat bar 97) needs power and projection within the *pianissimo* dynamic stipulated, and the chord that follows – in the most resonant part of the instrument – has to be realised on the threshold of silence if the overall balance is not to be spoiled. In both, the left-hand needs to come away from the keyboard quickly, and the speed with which this is realised requires experimentation and care.

Even elementary-level pianists can use the principles described above to experiment with. In this way, excerpts from masterpieces in the piano literature open up more possibilities for all players.

Inner voices

The technique of projecting subsidiary notes and lines within textures is of course loosely related to the study of polyphony on the piano. Sadly, it is often overlooked in practice. This is a great pity, because so often it is precisely the projection of 'hidden' melodies, unusual dissonances, appoggiaturas and subsidiary motifs that transforms bland play-throughs into deeply felt, meaningful performances. Of course, it takes years of patient practice to master the art of inner voicing before coming anywhere near emulating the achievements of a Jorge Bolet or Shura Cherkassky in this area. However, the basic polyphonic exercises outlined earlier apply equally well for projecting expressive inner voices in all kinds of contexts, and as such there is nothing to stop experimentation in all kinds of contexts from happening at once – whatever level the player happens to be at! Changing the perspective of a piece by adjusting the hierarchy via imaginative voicing can be extremely inspiring. It can transform your entire attitude to practice and dramatically improve your playing.

Whenever pianists discuss voicing there is every likelihood that the opening
of Beethoven's Piano Concerto No.4 in G major, Op.58 will be mentioned. The
noble, spiritual beauty of this magical opening is extremely hard to capture
without affectation:

Though potentially frustrating, it is certainly beneficial to isolate this phrase,
highlighting each line within it in turn. But because this is such a considerable
challenge, perhaps the opening of the slow movement in Beethoven's first
concerto is more approachable for less experienced players:

Its melody line is set at a higher tessitura than the accompanying chords in
the bass, and this makes it comparatively easy to control. Try highlighting each
strand of its opening in turn, taking care to relax and savour every sound to
the full.

The benefits of a daily contrapuntal warm-up routine like this tend to overspill
into all the practising that follows. Pianists are uniquely placed to celebrate and
enjoy the multi-textured nature of music. Polyphonic awareness is certainly
fun – but it is also a godsend in many respects. You will find that the ability
to highlight subsidiary strands in textures makes your memory much more
reliable. You will begin whistling and humming bass lines from memory in
the shower in the morning, and find that your repertoire sticks inside your
head more vividly when you are away from the piano. And from a technical
perspective, focus on secondary melodies can take your mind away from
treacherous technical pitfalls. If you are inwardly singing a lower voice placed
directly below a treacherously hard right-hand line, your brain will be relieved
from worrying about the technical problems, and your playing will be more
calm and confident as a result. But above all, working on inner voices takes the
stress and strain away from practice – it forces you to slow down and savour,
'gloat' over and project special intervals, wonderful dissonances within
chords and extraordinary inner-melodic threads. Practising inner melodies
can be a voyage of discovery, transforming familiar music into something
fresh and original.

Inner voices in practice

Though an awareness of inner voicing can be cultivated from the earliest stages of development, it truly comes into its own in the high romantic repertoire. Perhaps no composer illustrates its possibilities more than Sergei Rachmaninov. Hailed by some pianists as 'the Russian Bach', his extraordinary writing for piano can overwhelm even the most confident of players. In virtually every page of his oeuvre it is possible to find subsidiary *cantabile* lines that need to be isolated, exaggerated and enjoyed to the full. This is a key strategy if your aim is to conquer, for instance, the overwhelmingly rich chordal sequences at the centre of the slow movement of his third concerto. It is important, too, in the (relatively straightforward) realisation of the second subject in the first movement of his celebrated second concerto. Here the often neglected bass line can really mesmerise and set the atmosphere. When played with melodic expression and sensitive shading, it can match the beauty and shape of the famous right-hand melody it supports. In the much later *Rhapsody on a Theme of Paganini*, Rachmaninov's specific and detailed instructions on the score are crucial to the voicing and balancing of textures in most of the slow central variations. By carefully observing note lengths and accentuation markings throughout this work students have a ready-made course in inner voicing from one of the greatest pianists of all time at their disposal. Sadly, all too few tend to take the necessary time to follow exactly Rachmaninov's detailed requests.

Scriabin's writing for piano also demands exceptional contrapuntal awareness. Vladimir Horowitz's performance of Scriabin's early C sharp minor étude, Op.2 No.1, remains a textbook illustration of the enormous emotional depth that can result from the hands of a master pianist when he catches contrapuntal fire in performance. It is also worth mentioning Percy Grainger, who was perhaps more explicit than anyone else with regard to voicing. Grainger went as far as to enlarge noteheads so as to illustrate more precisely which voices he wished to have projected. This can be seen in his masterly transcription of the *Irish Tune from County Derry*.

The pitfall of inner voicing is that it can lead to affectation and artifice rather than integrity and honesty in performance. The Classical repertoire in particular can suffer from a ponderous over-statement of a subsidiary line. It would be unthinkable to over-project the bass octaves at the beginning of the 'Moonlight' sonata, for example, or to try to be clever with the bass hand in Mozart's 'Rondo alla Turca'. But creativity and poetry will thrive if performers listen carefully to the tonal balance as they play, and always inwardly sing their inner melodies. The examples below from the standard nineteenth-century repertoire are very similar but serve to illustrate the differences between affectation and creativity. In Schumann's theme (the opening of his celebrated *Études Symphoniques*, Op.13) it is possible to experiment with many possibilities of tonal hierarchy, provided there is a melodic thread in each voice:

However, the Schubert theme (opening of the second movement of his *Wanderer Fantasy*, Op.15) should be handled with greater caution:

This is a direct reference to 'The Wanderer' song, and as such it demands a vocal approach in performance. The pianist really has only two choices: to project the soprano line or to project the tenor line an octave below. Anything else would simply distort the character of the music.

Pedalling and texture

Finally in this chapter, an all-too-brief introduction to an enormous subject: the role of the sustaining pedal in texture. Examples will come from concert repertoire, as we are dealing mainly with sophisticated refinement of style. Nonetheless there are principles that can be applied to all levels of playing here. Pianists can emphasise the melody line over the harmonies by pedalling in such a way that the melodic contours are given emphasis. Alternatively, and traditionally, pedal changes can occur with the harmonies, or the emphasis in practice can be with the changes in the bass line. These decisions are largely about emphasis in practising, and players of all levels should re-emphasise and adjust the tonal balance through experiments whilst practising. Ultimately, it is up to the performer to decide whether the bass, the melody or the accompaniment in a given passage requires enhancement by using the sustaining pedal. Once the decision is taken whether to emphasise melodic flow or inner energy (this could be the case in the opening bars of Mendelssohn's E minor Prelude and Fugue, Op.35 No.1) or bass-line intensity (personally, I would always have the bass notes in mind when considering pedalling in the first page of the Bach/Busoni Chaconne in D minor, BWV 1004), decisions over how slow or fast pedal changes need to be made become much easier. Your ears become your guide. If you choose to pedal through harmonic changes, it follows that the less important strands in the texture have to be thinned down so that the most vital ingredients are given the chance to shine. Let's conclude with three fascinating and contrasted examples.

'Over-pedalling' and the Viennese masters

Comment should be made of the 'open pedal' four bars in the recapitulation of the first movement in Haydn's 'English' C major Sonata, Hob. XVI:50:

Though written in 1791 for an instrument quite different from today's Model D Steinway, it is possible to follow Haydn's pedal directions exactly if one depresses the sustaining pedal only a quarter of the way down at the most. And by experimentation with tonal balancing between the hands, it is possible to achieve a magical reverberant glow in performance. The famous 'blurred' Beethoven sonata passages are also worth considering in this context, such as the opening bars in the finale of the 'Waldstein' sonata, Op.53, and the recitative bars in the first movement of the 'Tempest' sonata, Op.31 No.2. Here, too, performers frequently shy away from attempting the pedalling shown in the score, simply because they are reluctant to experiment with tonal balancing between the hands or the level to which the pedal is depressed.

Holding the line

It is also possible to use long-pedalling as a means of sustaining the melodic line simply by 'under-playing' non-harmonic notes in melodic passages or chords, such as in the last four bars of Chopin's D flat major Nocturne, Op.27 No.2:

Sometimes it is wonderful to achieve a 'duality' of varied short musical punctuation through 'fussy' execution with the hands, while simultaneously pedalling straight through a particular passage with no changes from the right foot. This works especially well in the works of Debussy.

Visionary aura

Bach's Chromatic Fantasia and Fugue in D minor, BWV 903 (bars 36–45), has long been a challenge for pianists in terms of right-foot control:

If you choose Busoni's radical transcription of the work, then the whole gamut of pedal colour becomes available to you, including overlapping harmonies via long-pedalling at extreme chromatic moments, and evoking reverberation appropriate to a Gothic cathedral to bring to the fore an organ sonority in all its magisterial glow. While some performers seem to have been influenced here at least in part by Busoni (hear Alfred Brendel's visionary recording on Philips), an increasing number opt for finger-pedalling, whereby most of the overlapping is accomplished without the need for much footwork at all. However, in the emotionally charged quasi-improvisatory harmonies of bars 33–42 and 45–50, there is a real interpretive need for extraordinary qualities, and many pianists will here use 'pedal-*crescendo*', whereby as the music moves towards larger arpeggiation and more widely spaced chords, greater and greater sustaining pedal is used. I begin with finger-pedalling only in bar 33, then employ 'pedal-dabs' on selected pivotal notes around bars 37–40, before pedalling every beat from bar 40. Finally, in bars 48–50 the pedal is held for considerably longer, although I would never depress it further than half-way down.

Part 3

'S'x4

10 Speed

'S'x4

Speed, Strength, Stamina and Security – or 'S'x4 – forms the part of piano technique most readily associated with physicality. In *The Foundations of Technique*, I discussed 'music as sport' (Chapter 9) and suggested a series of exercises for developing athletic reflexes (Appendix 3). Though 'S'x4 overlaps with much that has already been discussed, we need now to go into greater detail and consider further options in order to apply successfully various techniques to the repertoire. In practice, it makes sense to focus on each aspect of 'S'x4 independently, even if this will inevitably lead to some repetition in the text. Indeed, dovetailing from one chapter to the next here is essential for proper understanding, as all four topics have much in common.

Telescopic rhythmic work with the metronome

The 'musical binoculars' exercises with the metronome to develop rhythmic awareness (see Chapter 2, p.23–5) can be re-used effectively here to develop speed, strength and stamina with a different emphasis in turn. Indeed, it is useful to play a scale, five-finger exercise or piece at a consistent tempo four times, but to adjust the metronome on each repetition so that it is in effect beating out semiquavers, then quavers, crotchets and minims. How can this help you play faster? The answer is all to do with emphasis and effort. It is extremely hard to play quickly when you are consciously aware of lots of vertical up–down, up–down movements. When you work telescopically with the metronome in any exercise, try to feel that each metronomic tick equates to a single up–down movement. Clearly, it should be much easier to play eight semiquavers with a feeling of one single thrust (or one metronome tick as a minim) rather than to play with eight different movements at the same speed. This is very similar to elementary conducting technique: no one would ever dream of conducting an 'Allegro molto' movement in 6/8 with six beats per bar. Apart from the obvious fact that it is much harder to move quickly when trying to make six rather than two movements per bar, conducting six beats in each bar would in all likelihood lead to injury! Just as a sensible conductor will mark each 6/8 bar with two beats – or even just one in very fast tempos – so a well-schooled pianist will feel that it is groups of notes rather single semiquavers that need to be depressed at any given moment. It is clear that working in this manner makes it possible to tackle Czerny studies, finales of Mendelssohn concertos, toccatas and much else from all styles and periods with a greater sense of comfort and control.

Beware of accents!

The telescopic principle emphasises the need to play with as few heavy accents as possible. This is an important rule of thumb to constantly recall as you strive to play faster. Clearly, horizontal flow is important when developing velocity, and any unnecessary vertical movements should be avoided or at least limited. Accentuation takes time and effort and slows everything down, and is therefore in general counter-productive.

Beware of physical *legato*!

Overlapping physically with the fingers between notes, and indeed holding on to notes for much longer than their written value, is an important aspect of technique that has been discussed previously.[32] Whilst the benefits of physical *legato* for sound production and a sense of security cannot be overstated, the approach is clearly not at all helpful if your priorities are to play quicker. I am indebted to a former student, Eddie Miles, for reminding me of this, as well as for pointing out what should be (but often is not) obvious: 'Clinging onto notes unnecessarily will slow down a performance tempo. Similarly trying to maintain *legato* where *legato* is not detectable also prevents the fastest tempos.'[33]

Perhaps mainstream piano pedagogy fails to stress the importance of releasing notes in order to find velocity and élan at the keyboard.[34] A possible reason for this could be the vital emphasis that must be placed on developing a beautiful tone and *cantabile*. *Staccato* and quick release of notes is certainly not helpful if you are striving to produce vocal qualities. However, it is interesting to remember that Busoni's monumental collection of exercises (his so-called *Klavierübung*) has an exhaustive selection of studies and exercises devoted to the *staccato* touch. Through practising and exploring *staccato* touches in the ways suggested earlier,[35] fluency and freedom of movement can certainly be encouraged and developed. Of course, teachers frequently refuse to teach *staccato* because it can lead to stiffness and tension – but I would equally argue that stiffness and tension could arise from attempting to play quickly whilst using the *legato* touch! Clearly, it is best to develop all the basic touches from the first stages onwards of piano playing. Care and attention should ensure that nothing is physically damaging in articulation – whichever touch is chosen.

Beware of bedding the keys!

In Chapter 5, the exploration of 'key-bedding' provided a means of producing vividly different colours from even the same dynamic level. To achieve maximum sonority and richness of tone, it is clearly advisable to 'dig like a

---

32 *The Foundations of Technique*, Chapter 7, p.38.
33 Private email from Eddie Miles, January 2015.
34 Ibid. 'Over the past 14 years, I have had the benefit of one-off or short groups of lessons with many concert pianists. Out of the 30 or so I have encountered only one (the late Mark Ray) kept on obsessively to me about releasing notes. I wondered why. Obviously I accept that I may be more prone to holding on notes than other students may but I suspect this was a reflection on his own training as a pianist. Perhaps this aspect is something that needs some publicity.'
35 See *The Foundations of Technique*, Chapter 6 and Appendix 3.

miner' and ensure that your fingers completely depress every key – bedding them onto the wood below the keyboard. However, if the priority is to play as fast as possible (or at least to play at a faster tempo), then key-bedding is very unhelpful. Playing on the surface of the keys will immediately make it much easier to increase speed. Experiment by practising five-finger exercises and scales with as light a touch as possible. Indeed, it can be fascinating to try to play loudly with a sense of fully bedding all the notes, then to continue at the same level of volume but ensure that the keys are not fully depressed. Find the level at which notes begin to speak, then experiment until you can control touch to the extent that you can play a scale in its entirety using only the shallowest levels of key depression. You should find that your fingers will naturally move towards your body as the velocity builds up. If this is not the case, it is advisable to revise the principles of the 'scratch *staccato*' touch outlined earlier.[36]

Avoid unnecessary changes of position

Changing hand position slows down your playing. If you want to play quickly, avoid using too many thumbs when you finger a scale run or an arpeggiated flourish. Fingering two-octave scales 1-2-3-4-5-1-2-3-4-5-1-2-3-4-5 will work if you avoid a *legato* touch and have mastered lateral movement.[37] There will be more on fingering in Chapter 16, but for the moment it should be noted that fingering that is not symmetrical between the hands is often more laborious and difficult to bring off fluently in practice. If you want to play quickly, use fingering between the hands that makes use of symmetry and simple mirror-like patterns.

Concluding remarks

It has been commented that the brain cannot process more than a certain number of notes at a time (apparently fifteen per second).[38] Therefore, with the exception of *glissandos*, this is the maximum speed at which we should play! In practice, we can create the illusion of playing much faster than we actually are simply by making sure that our articulation and rhythm are as lucid and solidly projected as possible.

Building up speed requires courage – you cannot afford to be frightened and inhibited by the possibility that you may make mistakes. 'Letting go' can mean less anxiety over individual notes and more concern for groups of notes, executed in one single arm-thrust movement. Using the pedal can certainly help you to realise this: if you keep the pedal down throughout a flourish of semiquavers, it is easier to feel that the notes belong together.

As with all the technical concerns examined so far, stiffness and poor posture should be avoided at all costs. If your wrists, shoulders, elbow or neck are tense,

36 Ibid., Chapter 6, p.34.
37 Ibid., Chapter 5, pp.30–31.
38 I am indebted to Eddie Miles for this information.

you are denying yourself the opportunity to let go and move freely. Take regular breaks as you practise and always take time to review your posture and set-up at the instrument.

As you strive to increase the speed of a particular passage through repetitive work, it can of course be helpful to use the metronome. In addition to patiently and slowly inching your way up from crotchet = 60 to crotchet = 120+, it may be helpful to work in small units of notes. Try playing one beat up to tempo and the next half speed, then reverse the process. Isometric rhythmic practice extends this principle, allowing you to move for only a few notes at a time up to tempo before resting on longer notes.[39] In terms of the physical and mental processing of notes, it is most helpful to look out for chordal shapes and sequences in the music. Being aware of patterns is essential if you wish to play fluently. Speed will also be much easier to build up if you can memorise your music. Even short-term memory is helpful when it comes to fluency in playing. Above all, remember to let go of notes after they have been played!

39   See *The Foundations of Technique*, pp.49–51.

11 Strength

In *The Foundations of Technique* the issue of strength in technique was addressed from different angles. Five-finger exercises and scale practice were cited as excellent ways of developing technique in general, including strength; and considerable time was spent discussing basic ways of developing finger strength and brilliance.[40] The question 'how much strength does it take to depress a piano key?' may be answered quickly with 'not that much!', but in a sense, it is the wrong question for what this present chapter is all about. *The Foundations of Technique* also established that strong articulation, clarity and sparkling sonorities are achieved through excellent coordination and focus. It emphasised the need to build up your playing via the use of the metronome as a proverbial treadmill, as well as examining ways in which isometric rhythms, accents and *staccato* flicks and scratches can all 'strengthen' finger work and so produce sounds that are more convincing, clear and penetratingly articulate. Strength in technique can then be extended through practising demanding virtuoso études, which will do wonders for 'S'x4 – provided practising is always done with intelligence and understanding.

We need now to go further and find ways of producing pianism that can stand up in the largest of halls and against the strongest of orchestras. Putting technique into practice with conviction means being able to perform publically with the requisite strength expected by audiences, international juries, conductors and critics the world over. It is never too early to start aiming for these dizzy heights. Indeed, it can be argued that it is every piano teacher's duty to ensure that all their pupils are aware of the fact that the instrument they are playing is designed to be performed in a large public venue. Too many beginners are timid and frightened when they play. Often it seems as though they are cowed by neighbours or siblings into practising quietly so as not to disturb the peace. This is a great shame as it leads to a style of playing that is both apologetic and unmemorable. The overwhelming majority of pieces in the solo repertoire were not designed as background fare for coffee houses. Teachers should remember this and encourage students to open up. Pianists of all levels and abilities should enjoy developing their potential to play with strength and projection.

Keyboard dives

In terms of brute force at the instrument, much depends on the speed with which you can depress the keys. This can be developed through fast movements from above the keys in the following eccentric, but highly effective, exercise: experiment by raising your hands to a dangerously high level above the keyboard (as much as three feet above the notes!) before quickly thrusting downwards in a single, unstoppable movement to play a chord or single note.[41]

40 *The Foundations of Technique*, Chapter 8.
41 This was initially demonstrated to me in private lessons with Ronald Stevenson.

When I ask students to do this in lessons they immediately assume that they will be unable to play with accuracy. Happily, this always proves to be a bad assumption: if they look at the note(s) they are about to play, and if they can dive downwards from the high initial starting position without hesitation or deviation en route, then accuracy is always a certainty! I find that diving down onto a note is extremely useful when trying to give real pizzazz and bite to an individual note or group of notes: if you play a run or flourish of notes in a single, diving movement from way above the keyboard, the articulation will be stronger and more vibrant. This is similar to the 'telescopic' technique of practising groups of notes as described in Chapters 2 and 10. The point here is that one single, fast movement from above the keyboard provides stronger sounds than many smaller movements from further down. Certainly, the sound quality that arises from high diving is more vibrantly charged than that from playing which begins nearer the surface of the keyboard! It is worth practising by diving down onto the keys from different heights and in different contexts. Eventually you will become aware of what works best in different musical contexts.

Projection

The ability to project with sufficient tonal strength and carrying power is an important area of technique but is clearly often neglected or overlooked. Indeed, at even the highest of levels inexperienced young artists – no matter how gifted and well-schooled – can fail in this department: one of the most common complaints from jury members in international competitions is that finalists often fail to be heard when playing concertos with a full symphony orchestra. Perhaps this is because it is all too easy to consider the sounds one produces in practice or in a piano lesson exclusively in relation to the dimensions of the practice studio or teaching room. It has to be said that one of the great drawbacks of conventional one-to-one teaching is that the venue chosen for lessons tends to be small. Even the most understanding of teachers will not be able to offer advice that is unaffected all the time by the acoustics of a domestic setting or conservatoire teaching room, if that is where the lessons usually take place. Let's examine some of the ways in which projection can be developed on a daily basis – in even the smallest of rooms.

The performer has to be aware of their posture, declamatory power and timing at the instrument. He or she has to become a great actor in approach if their message is to be conveyed and carried through beyond the footlights. It is all too easy for inexperienced pianists to assume that everything they are thinking about as they play will automatically be heard by the audience. Because there is so much to think about in piano playing, young players often forget that it takes a considerable amount of physical effort and will power to project changes of colour, atmosphere, shaping of phrases and characterful rhythm. To simply 'think' of a change in colour is not enough: the successful performer needs to know how effective their adjustments to sound are as they play. They need to do much more than mentally recall the details on the printed text. To be completely aware of just how many – or how few – of their interpretive ideas are actually travelling and arriving safely at the back row of an auditorium is an essential aspect of a performer's technique.

In order to project contrasted dynamics and colours, it is useful to practise many possibilities in isolation prior to refining particular passages in the music. In terms of dynamics, it is helpful to try using once more the dynamic exercise with the opening of Schubert's B flat Sonata, D.960 (see Chapter 5, p.47). Of course, you can try out this exercise with many different passages, aiming to clearly show up to eight different dynamic levels in eight successive repetitions of the same phrase.

If you aspire to perform in an auditorium, it makes sense to get at least some experience of playing and practising in them – preferably during piano lessons, so that your teacher can help you to project in the way you will have to when performing to an audience. When you can convincingly project to the back of a large auditorium the same passage played at **_ppp_**, **_pp_**, **_p_**, **_mp_**, **_mf_**, **_f_**, **_ff_** and **_fff_**, then you know that you are fully in command of your sonic range. Learning to do this usually takes a considerable amount of time and effort. It is important to engage the help of fellow musicians who can sit at the back of the concert hall and provide instant feedback on how your playing is coming across in the full spectrum of dynamics. Make sure that you do at least occasionally have piano lessons in a concert hall, as you will inevitably find that your teacher notices things in a larger venue that would in all likelihood have been undetectable in a conventionally smaller teaching studio. Let's now move on to consider how pedalling, fingering and touch can influence projection.

Pedalling

In a general sense, there is a danger of being too polite and careful in the use of the sustaining pedal. Pedalling that adopts careful changes on each change of harmony –and this is a standard approach recommended by basic textbooks on piano technique – can lead to a lack of power, especially (but not exclusively) in concertos. I recommend lots of experimentation with pedal changes, making sure that a reliable listener is situated in the auditorium for instant feedback. Of course, I should mention here with caution that the acoustics of empty auditoriums are totally different from those of halls filled with many people, and that ultimately it is only through experience that pianists can learn how to cope with pedal techniques that 'work' in halls both filled and unfilled!

By several published accounts, Vladimir Horowitz's teaching frequently mentioned the need to adjust pedalling for the concert hall from pedalling that works well in smaller settings. It never fails to amaze me just how vulgar pedalling often has to become in order to succeed in the concerto repertoire. In the opening of Prokofiev's first piano concerto, Op.10, for example, it is often impossible to hear the piano's double octaves at all, particularly if the pedalling is tastefully changed by the well-intentioned soloist with each octave and harmonic shift. Experience here has shown that if the sustaining pedal is held down and left unchanged for the whole of the first page of this concerto in a symphony hall that seats thousands, the piano will be heard. Moreover, the pedalling will not sound blurred. On the contrary, the resulting sonorities will be clear and articulate!

Space forbids more than a few further comments on pedalling as a means towards projection. However, it must be mentioned that catching and holding pedal-point notes in the third pedal is a good way of building up sonority. This can be seen in the opening of Saint-Saëns's second piano concerto, Op.22, where the first octave G can be held down for the entire opening page.

Fingering

Along with pedalling, choice of fingering is a vital factor for projection. If power and strength are priorities, it makes sense to use as little of the fourth finger as possible. For instance, runs in Mozart concertos often fail to convince with standard fingering such as 5-4-3-2-1-3-2-1 (C major descending scale, one octave) but will glow with greater authority with a simple adjustment to 5-3-2-1-5-3-2-1. When strength matters, it is often better to use no more than a couple of fingers at a time, giving each digit lots of weight and force. Therefore, I recommend using only fingers 1 and 2 for maximum power in a scale run of five or even six notes. Lateral fingering and constant curiosity are essential for pianists who wish to remain focused on the desire to increase the range of their technical possibilities at the instrument. For this reason, fingering should never stand still!

The sonorous single descending right-hand line in the slow movement of Grieg's celebrated piano concerto in A minor, Op.16 (bars 45–7, example below) truly blooms with golden sonority and tonal depth when it is executed exclusively by the thumb alone, with full body weight behind each note. To use several fingers in succession in this passage somehow never quite feels the same. The use of the thumb alone in examples similar to the Grieg can be equated to using successive single down-bows for individual notes in a violin piece in order to give each one particular emphasis:

Touch

Projection is particularly relevant in Debussy's unique tonal universe, and many passages in his oeuvre require special pianistic approaches that would appear to contradict conventional textbook pianism. This is certainly true of the opening bars in 'La Cathédrale engloutie' from *Préludes* Book 1 (see p.15), which really takes flight with wistful magic and mystery when its opening chords are 'lifted' out of the keyboard. To use overlapping textbook *legato* here would result in sonorities that remain earthbound or even academic in realisation. It would also make it hard to use long, evocative pedalling. But by literally lifting up your hands 15–20 centimetres above the keyboard for each chord whilst using relaxed arms and wrists – along with synchronised wrist/hand movements – it is possible to produce much of the sparkle and individuality of tone that are required within Debussy's *sotto voce* dynamic range. The sustaining pedal can then be used with less prosaic changes, enhancing the atmosphere considerably.

Bars 98–9 of Liszt's 'Harmonies du soir' from his twelve *Études d'exécution transcendante* show how two completely different technical approaches can be used in the same passage, in order to really project tonal excitement and contrast with a strong dynamic impact in even the largest of concert venues:

Firstly, the octaves at the bottom and top of the texture should be executed with full body weight. The back initially 'pushes' each double octave into the keys at a 45° angle, then the arms and wrists lift each octave up in preparation for the next one. The physical sensation in a group of 'spinning octaves' like this one should feel circular, as though the arms and wrists are moving in a consistent, naturally looping movement. The sparkle and tonal buzz will increase if you raise your octaves higher and faster. Meanwhile, excitement in the second element of this example – the repeated chords at the centre of the texture – also depends largely on the speed and distance by which you can lift off the notes from the keyboard. In this case, we are dealing with less arm movement and much more concentration from the wrists. This rapid 'vibrato' movement can prove extremely effective with repeated chords so that practice here needs to concentrate mainly on relaxed coordination of the wrists.

12 Stamina

The ability to maintain a fast speed for more than a few bars in a virtuoso piece develops primarily from regular and intelligent work in the practice studio. For most, stamina needs careful nurturing, and this applies equally to sustaining an extreme dynamic level or maintaining an obsessive rhythmic motif over a long period. Sadly, many amateur players who are returning to playing the piano after extended periods away from the instrument can end up injuring themselves through over-enthusiasm and obsessive and sudden work. Though music is not the same as sport, there are some basic similarities. If you have done no exercise other than a moderately paced walk for the first forty years of your life, it would be madness to suddenly run seven successive 10km distance races for a week. You would end up in hospital! However, this is exactly what many amateur pianists are doing musically when they suddenly restart playing. The get so excited and carried away by the sudden opportunities available to them that they sit at pianos for longer than they have ever done before, playing as loud as possible. Little wonder that they quickly end up feeling exhausted. Over the years I have learnt to advise students of all ages that they need to pace themselves and 'listen to their bodies' in order to avoid over-strain, tired muscles or inflamed tendons.

Playing for extended periods requires both concentration from the player and an understanding of the most comfortable and effective means of executing that technique. Stamina is virtually impossible until technique has become a part of the subconscious; and without a natural ease, stiffness, stress and tiredness can seep into 'difficult' music, even in short passages.

Building your stamina using the metronome

Throughout *The Foundations of Technique*, an emphasis was placed on playing with comfort as well as on the slow, patient build-up of coordination and understanding. Indeed, slow, methodical practice is a highly effective way of building up your stamina. Like an athlete, the key is to start slowly and increase your 'fitness' level gradually. Once you can play a given passage comfortably and with coordination at a slow tempo, you can move on in several ways. The most common way is to set the metronome at the lowest possible pulse, play a page, and then move the metronome up a notch and repeat the process. If you keep a close eye on your finger movements and check for tension and 'bad performance practice', there is nothing to prevent you from working up the metronome scale towards a superhuman tempo! The drawback with this approach becomes apparent when you reach your optimum speed, because frustration and anxiety can easily lead to increased stiffness and you can end up undoing all the good work done in the slower tempos. To combat this, return to a slower tempo and gradually build up again. Remember: quiet, calm, slow practice is the key to building up your stamina levels, so if you feel things getting out of control, return to a slower tempo until you are comfortable to move up.

Building up your stamina through small units

As a complement or alternative to the metronome method, I recommend working up to tempo – or even exceeding tempo – in very small units of four, six or eight notes. The trick is to execute each unit in one movement of the hand, and then to gradually increase the length of each unit into four-bar, eight-bar and finally sixteen-bar units. This is a remarkably effective and swift way to make progress with your stamina levels, and as an extra exercise, try repeating each unit with your eyes shut. This will help you to both assimilate and memorise the notes.

'Little and often' is certainly the best means of increasing facility in pieces written in constant semiquavers. Repertoire of this nature provides an excellent means for building endurance at all levels, as in the example below: Bach's famous 'lute' Prelude, or Little Prelude in C minor, BWV 999 (a piece frequently attempted by grade 4–5 players). You can sing the words 'Bach, J.S. Bach' to all of the left-hand melody as a means of remaining focused, and use a little rotary movement on the oscillating right-hand thirds, as well as 'touch and press' weight by pivoting on the right-hand middle C notes. However, begin work on the piece in single-beat scraps. Play each beat (four semiquavers of music) up to speed but make sure that you take long breaks between each one. When you can cope with this, take two beats and do the same. Then try whole bars, phrases and finally the whole study.

Re-using the telescopic method and other approaches

By practising 'telescopically' you can dramatically increase your stamina. As we have already discovered (in Chapters 2, 10 and 11), the telescopic method involves setting a metronome so that each 'tick' corresponds with different note values. For example, take an étude in semiquavers, set the metronome to 160, and practise so that each metronome tick corresponds with each semiquaver. Once you have mastered this, set the metronome to 80 and play the same passage at the same tempo, but think of the quavers as you play rather than the semiquavers. Then set the metronome to 40 and think instead of the crotchets. The aural–finger facility you will learn from this vitally important exercise will stand you in good stead when it comes to playing fast passages with calm authority. Instead of worrying about counting 16 semiquavers to every bar, you can calmly focus on four beats. In fast études, where the aim is to play like a hummingbird, extensive and complex figurations must be practised until no conscious thought is necessary for their safe execution.

Distracting agents

Psychologically, the pianist will have much more stamina when the going gets tough technically, if he or she can concentrate on the melodic notes in a passage rather than on every accompanimental semiquaver. Training the inner ear to inwardly concentrate on a relatively slow-moving melodic shape, whilst physically the hands are executing thousands of demisemiquavers, is extremely useful. Not only will the phrasing of the passage in question be beautiful; such an approach also means that there is no time to worry about inaccuracies. Make all melodies 'distracting agents' in performance and you will be amazed at how your confidence will soar!

Lateral movement for groups of notes

The repetition of too many down–up movements at the piano within a concentrated time limit can be extremely tiring. If we wish to play comfortably for longer stretches of time, it makes sense to avoid over-emphasising individual notes with heavy accents. We have already mentioned that too many thumb position shifts can make it challenging to build up speed. In a similar way, too many vertical movements can be tiring for the player, making it hard to keep going. This is certainly true in many of the famous transcendental studies. Of course, Chopin's 24 *Études* Op.10 and 25 stand as towering challenges to a pianist's stamina, and the ability to master them with coordination, ease and a minimum of tension and stiffness is worth striving for. Because these études are technically consistent throughout (each étude is presented entirely in the opening bar or bars), theoretically once the pianist has mastered the opening bars they have mastered the piece. Indeed, I often advise my students that their piano technique can be cultivated by learning thoroughly the first line of each Chopin étude! However, a lack of stamina can destroy this hypothesis immediately, so it is vital that progress on the Chopin études is made by gradually building up the velocity and length of each section you are practising (mini breaks between each section you are practising are essential). The B minor octave étude, Op.25 No.10 (see below, bars 5–7), is phrased in such a way that the performer is encouraged to think through groups of octaves in units of six, nine or more octaves at a time. Imagine that you are skimming a pebble over a river when executing a 'roll' of octaves, and stamina will become far less of a stumbling block in performance.

Rotary movement and arm weight

As you work to become stronger and more resilient over longer periods, remember two labour-saving devices: rotation[42] and the relaxed use of arm weight.[43] These were both discussed in *The Foundations of Technique* but are worth further mention here as they can certainly make it easier to sustain energy in taxing repertoire. This is most certainly the case in études such as Chopin's C minor Op.25 No.12 and Op.10 No.5 ('Black Keys'). Whereas arm weight can be used in the former to prevent tiredness and stiffness, the latter is often cited as a model example for showing the usefulness of rotary movement. Not for nothing did the legendary pedagogue Tobias Matthay recommend that technical woes could often be banished via rotation, surely one of the healthiest of technical approaches at the keyboard.

42   **Rotary movement** is one of the most comfortable ways of playing, as its successful execution requires complete freedom and a sense of 'letting go' as you rapidly swivel your lower arm/wrist in comfortable, oscillating movements that feel effortless. *The Foundations of Technique*, Chapter 7, p.44
43   **Arm weight** also takes the effort away from your fingers. If you can silently 'prepare' notes by touching them in advance with your fingers, then play the notes without lifting your fingers off the keys, you are using upper arm weight, and it is possible to feel that all of the energy and impetus for articulation can come from this 'weight' rather than from your knuckles and wrists. I would argue that this approach more than any other can lead to a healthy technique, and one where stamina ceases to be an issue at all. *The Foundations of Technique*, Chapter 5, p.28

13 Security

Mistakes

All too often, it seems that many serious piano students have an obsessive desire for accuracy as their strongest motivation in practice sessions. They spend hours upon hours working and re-working at challenging sections in their studies and concertos in order to produce blemish-free renderings in performance. They nag at their teachers, friends and parents about 'all the wrong notes' they drop, and sometimes they even hang around in the foyers of concert halls after wonderful concerts in order to complain about mistakes that they have just heard from wonderful and well-established artists! They become obsessed with mechanical perfectionism and move further and further away from the reasons we love music, live performance and artistry in its many guises.

'White' pianism

Perhaps this mechanical obsession is a reflection of the era in which we live, where heavily edited commercial recordings are the norm. But the origins of so-called 'white' pianism,[44] in which zero tolerance is expected in terms of minor fluffs/wrong notes, probably goes back to Busoni and Rachmaninov, great composer–pianists who had by all accounts infallible techniques. Their legacy was extended through iconic artists later in the last century, including Sviatoslav Richter and Arturo Benedetti Michelangeli. The tradition continues today with Maurizio Pollini. Richter, Michelangeli and Pollini have left us with a collection of exceptional recordings that stand as a great testament for future generations. The problem with their legacy is that students tend to focus on the least-interesting aspect of it – the mechanical accuracy – rather than on the remarkable artistry. This is extremely destructive, as an obsession with clean pianism alone is counter-productive in terms of artistic development. Indeed, there is a school of thought that believes in never mentioning mistakes in piano lessons: certainly, random slips from students (of course, all pianists miss notes from time to time!) should not be specifically pointed out by teachers who wish to nurture and develop vibrantly confident and creatively expressive students.

The sad thing about wrong notes is the more you worry and think about them, the more they tend to procreate. Ironically, the way to overcome untidy playing is to forget all about accuracy and focus with deep concentration and clarity on what you hope to achieve musically. When you understand what you want to do with every individual note and rest in your repertoire, you can then utilise your technical resources and make your dreams become realities.

---

44 I am indebted to Graham Scott, Head of the School of Keyboard Studies at the Royal Northern College of Music, for introducing me to this phrase: an expression used by professional pianists and teachers to describe an approach and style of playing that is entirely blemish-free, clean and generally without excesses in terms of exaggerated *rubato* and unusual voicings.

'Be Prepared'

When discussing accuracy and security, it makes sense to remember Robert Baden-Powell's famous Scouts motto: 'Be Prepared'. On a purely mechanical level, this means getting over notes in advance. If you can physically cover the keys before you depress them, you are in effect playing the notes twice: the first time silently; the second time for real. This approach should be experimented with in your entire repertoire. Of course, this is closely associated with the 'touch and press' approach to technique discussed extensively in *The Foundations of Technique*. I recommend re-studying scales and arpeggios, hands separately at first, ensuring that thumbs move quickly over notes well in advance of position changes, so that as soon as a thumb note is played, preparation for the next thumb note is underway. 'Jump practice' can be profitable for advance preparation too. As soon as you leap off one note in order to play the next, make sure that you arrive in advance. Literally touch the note you are about to play a split second before you allow the note to sound. Though pre-playing every note in your repertoire may not always be possible (or even musically desirable), it is an important skill to refine and develop. Keeping your thumbs constantly in touch with the keyboard (see *The Foundations of Technique*, p.27), and adopting a consistent economy of movement with fingers as close to the keys as possible, will certainly make piano playing easier, however much in advance the fingers are able to silently 'pre-play' notes.

Patience and repetition

Though I firmly believe in banning any direct verbal reference to 'wrong notes' in piano lessons, it is nonetheless vital for pianists of all ages and stages to do everything they can in practice to ensure that they are playing with the greatest amount of focus and precision. Throughout *The Foundations of Technique*, slow, patient and careful practising was cited as the best means of making progress. Previous chapters in this book also emphasise the need for pianists to develop their techniques via sensitive listening and intelligent understanding of the issues involved. Hand in hand with this approach is the need for repetition during practice hours. It is simply not enough to play accurately once or twice: the human brain needs time to assimilate information, and repetition plays an important role in the assimilation process. How repetitive work is tackled tends to divide pianists into two camps.

Mechanical drilling versus artistic sensitivity

On the one hand, students can be told to practise heavily in isometric rhythms, *fortissimo*, with little regard for the musical context or meaning, or even the dynamics on the page. They are told to aim for confidence and security, even though the end result has nothing to do with what they are trying to achieve musically. This is 'mechanical drilling' and can be viewed as the antithesis of creative practice.

In complete contrast is scenario two – 'artistic sensitivity' – where students are urged to practise for the musical result, with sounds in their inner ears. They are encouraged to strive for the magical, artistic vision. Practice can still utilise isometric rhythms and focus on small groups of notes played up to speed, and work can still be meticulous and fussy.

The problems with mechanical drilling are obvious, but the problems with artistic sensitivity are also quickly evident to anyone who has taught young pianists who simply do not yet have sufficient mechanical skills to cope with exposed pianism. Quite clearly, mindless mechanics are wrong, but equally wrong is vague artistry. Creative ideas in the practice room will not work unless they are backed up by a profound understanding of how to control sounds. It takes subconscious motor skills and coordination at a subliminal level for all the messages from teachers to sink in to the extent that they will always be reliable.

As suggested in *The Foundations of Technique* (Chapter 8), the answer is to find inspiration and celebration in the early stages of technical development in the 'music as sport' aesthetic, whilst remembering that listening always remains vital, and that music is so much more interesting and valuable than anything merely athletic. It is a myth to assume that fingers need to be 'built up' in terms of strength for X number of hours a day whilst the ears can switch off. Truly productive technical progress is as intellectually demanding (and potentially as emotionally draining) as any other kind of work at the piano. It is the combination of alert ears, physical relaxation/well being and imaginative/emotional receptivity that produces positive results with regard to accuracy at the instrument.

Control

Clearly, control in piano technique comes from having the clearest conception at all times of what you want to do, as well as a precise understanding of how to achieve this. Having 'control' in a concert situation means having energies in reserve. When it comes to actual performance, it is surely essential not to force the tone – nor to play at your optimum level of velocity. By always playing within your limits, you maximise your receptivity to creativity and cut back on risks of tension, anxiety and vulgarity. Remember the words of Matthay ('Never play faster than you can think') and Busoni ('I never play loudly'). The implication is that you should always feel it is possible to play louder and faster than you actually choose to do. In this way, control, poise and aristocratic effortlessness become so much easier to achieve.

Control begins with the left hand

Over the years I have witnessed in student performances more memory lapses and stumbles caused directly by left-hand insecurity than by anything else. In terms of memory, the left hand tends to be the one that gets left behind – and this fact can be all-too-cruelly revealed in concerts given by the inexperienced.

For this reason, it is vital that students are able to play their repertoire from memory with the left hand alone. It is one of the main ways in which security and confidence in performance can be achieved.

Of course, the right hand is much more 'glamorous' than the left, as it tends to have most of the melodic material in repertoire from the Baroque onwards. Yet the harmonic foundations, the basis on which most western music is formed, stem chiefly from the bass register. If you want to really understand how music unfolds and 'works', then it is usually much more revealing to play through the left hand on its own, rather than the right. This can be seen in countless works from the Romantic era in which the right-hand melody is the result of a harmonic sequence – the surface decoration and colour that rests on top of the musical bricks and mortar below. Think of the enormous stretches for which this applies in the Chopin Nocturnes, Mendelssohn *Songs without Words* and Schumann *Kinderszenen* pieces, to give but a few obvious nineteenth-century examples.

Naturally, most people find that their left hand is much less agile and coordinated than their right hand. Working to gain more facility, control and strength in the left hand takes time but should be constantly thought about. Away from the piano it can be useful to try doing everyday things with the left hand rather than the right (beating eggs, opening doors, even throwing and catching balls can be illuminating/helpful). It is certainly useful to spend a lot of time working at scales, arpeggios and broken chords with the left hand alone, and also to work at some of the wonderful repertoire that has been written exclusively for the left hand. (If the Ravel concerto is a little challenging at first, think about beginning with the Saint-Säens études or the two Scriabin Op.9 pieces.)

The excerpt below comes from Beethoven's Sonata in D major, Op.10 No.3, first movement, bars 23–6. It requires dexterity and concentrated coordination:

Too often students 'fudge' passages like this, perhaps half hoping that because it is in the left hand and not playing the melodic part no one will notice if it is not as perfect as it could be. Sadly, this is far from the case! Lack of control and focus here will destabilise the rhythm, potentially making the whole of this section of the movement incoherent. Clearly, it is vital to work religiously on a daily basis at articulation and evenness of touch until facility is second nature. Aim for a 'stereophonic' tonal balance so that the left hand is as important as the right as you practise. Of course, you will need to project the right hand over the left in this passage in performance, but you should make a point of building up control so that the bass part can stand on its own. Begin at a slow tempo and gradually increase the velocity. It can help to work in groups of four notes at a time, stopping for breaks on the fourth note. When you can do this, try stopping on every eighth note. Work in dotted rhythms. Try putting accents on the offbeats. Practise blind. Above all, keep listening and never give up until you can rattle off the left hand flawlessly on its own, from memory with your eyes closed.

In the next excerpt from Chopin – the Fantasie in F minor, Op.49, bars 84–7 – technical challenges are focused exclusively in the right-hand part:

However, the music's structural foundation is built up from the harmonic sequences in the left hand. If you downplay the left hand you are immediately depriving the listener of the crucial musical argument that moves the piece forward. You also make the technical task much harder for the right hand – there is nothing more challenging than feeling you are executing demanding figurations on the piano in one hand with no tonal support. However, if you allow this passage to reverberate with sonorities built from the glorious diminished-seventh chords of the left hand, then immediately you will feel less vulnerable and have more confidence. In fact, the way you shape the left hand in this passage has far-reaching effects on how exciting (or not) the passage is. Left-hand intensity and conviction are far more important than whether or not your right-hand flourishes are 100% clean.

'Safety last!'

'Safety last!' was Artur Schnabel's famous plea. If we aim for something musically safe, we risk limiting our horizons and stifling our creativity and ambitions. The really sad thing about students who obsess over accuracy is that the more they worry about it, the more inaccurate their playing tends to become. If you fill your head with negativity or concerns about what not to do, then you are immediately creating a mental image that will lead to lack of success in performance. Indeed, it could well be argued that technical control depends more on your mental state, your ability to concentrate and focus on the important things, than on any physical factor. If you are really excited and motivated by the musical *raison d'être* of a passage, technical coordination and control become so much easier.

Many pianists do not realise that mistakes can be turned by an artist into a precious art form in recital. Ronald Stevenson[45] once mentioned a performance by Mark Hambourg of Handel's 'Harmonious Blacksmith', in which the great pianist made an extremely noticeable slip in the first variation. On approaching the same passage on its repetition, Hambourg opted for a grandiose *ritardando* followed by a theatrical gesture, making the note in question special and pivotal as it arrived in the correct place second time round. The audience was thrilled! There are similar anecdotes about Liszt, who would famously incorporate split notes at the tops of arpeggios into new and beautiful arpeggios, so turning an 'inaccuracy' into a positive improvisational added plus. However, of course you need to be alert, imaginative and skilled as an improviser to cope with blemishes in this way. Unfortunately, too many of today's pianists are ill-equipped to cope with transposition, composition, sight-reading and harmonisation of melodies, and the lack of security in these vital areas makes them more vulnerable as performers, and so more worried and upset about potential disasters – which inevitably occur with ever-increasing frequency as they worry more and more about them.

Defeating this vicious circle of self-destruction can be difficult if it has been in place for many years, but it involves a return to basic values. We make music because we long to get away from the prosaic banalities of everyday existence. The notes we play take us to a better world and inspire us with aural imagery and reveries that become more alluring and intense the more we indulge.

When one sits down at the piano to practice, it is vital to remember this. If you are going to spend hours upon hours working at a sonata, there has to be a burning desire within you, a need to connect with the spirit of the music. Practising becomes a search for sonorities; an exploration and quest for sounds one longs to hear. The best practice often occurs when one totally loses oneself in this quest. Ideally, the sounds should be imagined away from the instrument and in advance of the practice session, so that the time spent at the instrument becomes experimental in the most acute way. Endless repetitions of minute passages become a search for the ideal balance; the most perfect shaping and pacing of a phrase turn; the most appropriate voicing one can achieve. It is easy to know when you are practising well, simply because you become unaware of the passing of time. Your ears become your sternest critics, and you strive and strive again for what you are trying to recreate.

Of course, nothing could be further from a quest for mechanical accuracy than what is described above. But the irony is that it is only by working in such a creative way that perfect control and precision, sustainable without pain and anguish, can hope to be achieved. The task of performing a demanding eighty-

---

45 Private conversation at the composer's home in West Linton, 1989.

minute recital programme from memory in front of an audience of several thousand becomes almost unbearable if it is reduced to an accuracy-level exercise. Mechanical perfection comes as a default privilege to artists who are after higher, loftier and more meaningful concerns. When such performers do drop the occasional wrong note, the mistakes tend to remain in the background. Listeners genuinely do not notice wrong notes from performers who have their priorities in the right place. How sad, then, that the reverse is also true: one need only attend the first round of any major international piano competition and hear playing that is 'safe' to understand this. Wrong notes from cautious players can become overwhelmingly obtrusive, as 'safe' playing inevitably shows up errors much more acutely than playing that has artistic integrity and substance.

So many examples could be given of great performances on disc and in concerts where wrong notes existed but with little negative impact. Space forbids mentioning more than a couple: anyone who attended Annie Fischer's remarkable London recitals at the end of her performing career will tell you that her playing was of extraordinary power and vision – despite generous numbers of split notes. On disc, Percy Grainger's last recording of the Grieg concerto was withheld for many years because 'powers that be' believed it to be too approximate, yet Benjamin Britten valued it highly and was convinced that it was a remarkable performance, as indeed it remains. One can return again and again to playing of this calibre because it captures the essence of Grieg's musical spirit. 'Safety last' indeed!

Summary

- Never mention wrong notes.
- Do not think of accuracy on its own.
- Look beyond mechanical control (or lack of it) in great recordings of the past.
- Be prepared!
- Have physical energy in reserve.
- Always ensure that the left hand is securely learnt.
- Constantly explore the 'touch and press' technique.
- Slow, patient, focused and concentrated practising with lots of repetition is essential.
- Safety last!

Part 4

Assimilation techniques

14 Sight-reading

> Sadly many of our pupils are poor readers. Often the reason is that
> they do very little reading, and as most people do not enjoy doing
> something they are not good at, they do even less. So we have to
> break this vicious circle and provide them with a structured course
> which will allow them to make good progress in reading.
> (*Christine Brown*)

Sight-reading angst is something that does not go away. Christine Brown's
words appeared in her excellent *Playing at Sight*, originally published in the
early 1960s but newly reprinted by Faber Music in 2008. Some would say that
things are worse now than ever before – simply because good sight-reading
skills are not now as important for musicians as they once were: in our hi-tech
age of websites, downloads, YouTube videos and iPods, 'instant accessibility' of
excellent recordings is taken for granted. This means that there is perhaps less
motivation for students than ever before to become skilled at sight-reading. If
a young pianist wants to find out what a Chopin Nocturne sounds like, chances
are he or she will not sight-read it. It is much easier to search for performances
on YouTube.

So why do we need good sight-reading skills in our technical armoury as
pianists? The most depressing answer I often hear when asking this question
in masterclasses and workshops is 'because it gives you a higher mark in
your examinations'. But that is not to dismiss the materialistic benefits of
sight-reading: there are mercenary reasons to be a good reader! In the music
industry, where time is in short supply, skilful sight-reading can be a lifesaver.
Poor sight-readers find it harder to assimilate notes, whereas those talented
in this field tend to grasp rudiments more quickly and move on to the more
artistic and less pedestrian levels of learning, and are generally able to get
much more enjoyment, more quickly, from their music-making than those who
struggle to decipher one note and rhythm from another. Clearly, good rather
than bad sight-readers will be asked to step in at short notice when someone
falls sick and the choir needs an accompanist at the last minute to step in. At a
student level as well as a professional level, sight-reading will certainly help to
pay the rent!

But the real reason why musicians need to be good at reading is that music is
a language: if you cannot read music easily, you are never going to understand
it properly. From personal experience, I find that composers are nearly
always fabulous readers. In the musical garden, they are always dirtying their
hands in the soil. Good sight-reading comes easily to those who are used
to manipulating dots and dashes on manuscript paper. It is by far the most
effective way of learning how to assimilate and understand logic, patterns and
progressions of every kind.

Positive steps towards mastering the technique of sight-reading

The first thing to realise is that success in this area comes from experience borne of practice as well as from a general awareness of music in a theoretical and practical sense. Good sight-readers understand about the rudiments of music and are able to instantly pick out chords, intervals, sequences, repetitions, extensions of ideas, harmonies, scales, and so on in music as they read it through for the first time. If you want to be a good sight-reader, work at the theory of music. You should also steep yourself in as much music as possible. The more music you know, the more you will be able to anticipate what will happen in the piece you are sight-reading. All the best readers are able to keep going as they play, knowing that there is a stylistic reason for why the music moves in a particular direction.

Along with theoretical awareness, technical facility is also crucial. There is simply no time for hesitations and stumbles as you read. Tied up closely with this is the need to not look at your hands whilst sight-reading. Pianists who look down tend to have stiff and angled necks, which in turn leads to bent backs and even to medical conditions, so I would argue that good posture is vital if you are serious about improving your sight-reading. 'Never look at your hands' is a good imperative to keep in mind at all times, and I have even suggested to students that they place small tablecloths over their hands as they play in order to stop them from looking. So keep your eyes glued on the printed copy rather than on your ten fingers, and try to look at the bass clef before the treble. Most music is harmonically biased, and you will do much better if you can grasp the chordal skeleton of a phrase as a prime objective before attempting to tackle its melodic contour. Do not get bogged down in detail – in order to 'see the wood from the trees' you need to practise turning notes into chords and complex runs into scale patterns, and seeing octave displacements as simple decorations of basic patterns.

The example below shows how the opening of Beethoven's 'Moonlight' sonata, No.14, Op.27 No.2, can be simplified into a succession of chords that would not be out of place as the naive basis for a straightforward pop song!

Try to adopt this 'telescopic' approach to all the music you are asked to play for the first time. Remember that there is very little need in practice to literally sight-read without first having had a glance at what you are asked to play for a few moments beforehand. Excellent training can be developed by analysing and playing silently in your head what you are about to play aloud. In a similar way, learning to memorise music away from the piano can certainly develop your sight-reading ability – as well as your aural skills and your musical imagination.

But good reading goes even deeper. It is essential to have excellent short-term memory skills. Your eyes should move along the page as you sight-read, and so it is vital to remember accidentals, the pulse, dynamics, pedal markings, and so on as you play. And, of course, in most practical situations you will find that you have at least half a minute to look over what you are about to play for the first time. So time spent memorising elements crucial to the piece before you start to play will pay dividends.

The hardest thing about sight-reading is the fact that you have to do so many different things simultaneously. You have no time to consider the pitches of each clef alone – your eyes need to be able to take in both at once. Rhythm needs to be logical and stable. Although it tends to be treated as less important than pitch by most aspiring players, the reverse is unquestionably true for all listeners! You also have to try to remember what key you are in, try to 'interpret', and try to capture dynamics, articulation and pedalling too. Multi-tasking skills indeed! Moreover, you also need a lot of insensitivity, because you cannot afford to stop and correct anything – ever. This is often too much for intensely musical, sensitive students to take, and they often end up disliking sight-reading solely because of this. Being able to see the wood rather than the individual trees is extremely important in sight-reading. A bird's-eye view can be cultivated by always remembering to focus on projecting the character of the piece you are reading through at sight. Never dissociate yourself from the emotional impact of the music you are attempting to recreate.

But perhaps the best way of all to develop excellent sight-reading is to do it with other musicians in chamber music, accompanying work and piano duets. Forcing yourself to play unfamiliar music with others is a surefire way to stimulate your reflexes and force you to keep going. For this reason, it is especially important for teachers to introduce duets into a student's programme of study as early as possible, and there are duets available from the pre-Grade 1 level upwards.

In terms of sight-reading tutor books, I particularly recommend those that opt for a holistic approach. Both Paul Harris[46] and Alan Bullard[47] have systematic approaches in their acclaimed graded series – a surefire way of improving your technical capabilities as a sight-reader. Harris's 'simultaneous learning' pedagogical approach aims to link each area of study at the instrument, so that aural energises theory work, which in turn has an impact on scales, arpeggios and repertoire – and as a result, sight-reading. Bullard makes a point of including not only standard tests in each chapter of his books, but also duets, exercises and even transposition and improvisation examples too. Transposition of exercises from the early grades should be encouraged as a means of improving pattern-recognition skills for students in the transitional and higher grades. Keyboard harmony and awareness of cadences and basic chordal progressions will undoubtedly help students to quickly assimilate

---

46 Paul Harris, *Improve your Sight-Reading!* (Faber Music, 2009).
47 Alan Bullard, *Joining the Dots* (ABRSM Publishing, 2010 and 2014).

music on the printed page at sight. It is all part of the broad understanding that lies at the heart of facility, awareness and coordination.

And what if even all of this proves inadequate? It is important to admit that the vast majority of students do not like sight-reading. Most people find sight-reading 'hell' and prefer to remain bad at it, no matter how often it is pointed out that the whole note-learning process ultimately becomes faster and more effective when their reading skills are good. We have already mentioned that it is not enough to expect progress from students by setting sight-reading exercises for them to plough laboriously through. Equally, it would be wrong to expect miracles to happen overnight simply by being positive and encouraging a 'keep going at all costs' approach. Sight-reading progress comes from a gradual awareness and understanding of music from many different perspectives. A background knowledge of theory, aural skills and improvisation, as well as an awareness of style via listening to lots of other music, will help, as will ensemble playing – not to mention the ability to tie in knowledge of scales with pieces and theory. The way forward is to turn sight-reading work into a regular habit – and to think of it not so much as 'work' but as play. Sight-reading exercises become much less dry and cerebral when viewed as musical games – fun on the same level as crossword puzzles. Humour and a sense of the ridiculous will not go amiss either as you soldier on. From personal experience in my own family, I can vouch for this – mixed with a liberal sprinkling of perseverance, encouragement and patience. Having coaxed four kids through from a dread of sight-reading to a level at which they can comfortably cope, I can only say that the journey for a parent and/ or teacher is a long, adventurous and varied one! Seeing children change from a viewpoint of complete hatred of sight-reading to a position where they genuinely enjoy doing their Christine Brown exercises each day is proof of the benefits of establishing a regularity of approach with this subject – provided it can be tackled with relaxed philosophical maturity and a sense of discovery. Young pianists generally morph into skilled sight-readers by sticking to the task in hand and approaching the challenge from different angles. If you own a Harris, Bullard or Brown course book, try writing down inside it the date each exercise is completed (often with a comment along the lines of 'very hard', 'easy' or 'odd'). Do not restrict yourself to merely playing through each example: try clapping, singing and making up words for each exercise too. Analytical study prior to the 'execution' of each exercise will also undoubtedly help – on intervals, key signatures, scales and ledger lines. Try previewing each exercise by playing the scale, chord and arpeggio of the key it is in, and attempt to improvise immediately after playing the exercise in a similar style. Recording your sight-reading and then listening back is an illuminating and profitable thing to do, as it makes you self-review and take note of where your strong and weak points were.

These are just some of the ways in which you can gradually build up your skill in this important area of technique. Sight-reading thrives where there is a sense of understanding, creativity, fun and stimulation. Students who are curious and desire to extend their horizons will always enjoy working and developing their sight-reading skills. We should all see sight-reading in terms of performance: whatever happens when we play through a piece for the first time, we need to keep going and always be as expressive in our efforts as we can. Above all, remain positive and upbeat when you sight-read. Progress in this area often comes when you least expect it to!

15 Textual fidelity

Follow the text!

If you wish to play with authority, conviction and style then it is essential, from the first stages onwards, that you follow all the instructions written into your music by the composer. Tempo indications, dynamics, pedalling, articulation and phrasing must be assimilated, carefully noted and then 'recreated' in sound as you practise. Processing and assimilating markings on the text can be mastered by developing specific techniques that can be applied in all kinds of contexts.

Do not think of the composer's markings as candyfloss: why would he or she take the effort to fill their music with details if they were not vital to the music? If the composer of your piece thought it was worthwhile taking the necessary time to write in precise dynamics and razor-sharp articulation, then the very least they deserve is respect from you – and an attempt to recreate exactly what is on the printed page in terms of dynamics, articulation and everything else.

In some cases it could well be argued that the dynamics and articulation marks on the score are actually more important than notes themselves. This is easy to understand when it is remembered that tone quality and the shaping of groups of notes (rather than notes in isolation) can be the most beautiful factors in a performance.

If one needs role models for inspiration on this subject, one could hardly do better than listen to the recorded legacies of three completely different past masters: Claudio Arrau, Clifford Curzon and Sviatoslav Richter. Each in their own unique way was a servant to Art, and their self-sacrifice, infinite patience and ceaseless effort in the practice studio led to enormous conviction on the concert stage. Both Arrau and Curzon evidently consistently stressed to students the need for scrupulous attention to all the markings on the copy, implying that interpretation should come primarily from the instructions on the music itself. And in a broader sense, it really is true that students are often told by their teachers to forget about their own whims and fancies in performance and simply 'do what is written'. This would appear to be a sentiment echoed by many twentieth-century composers, who almost seemed to call for a negation of 'personality' from performers by drastically increasing the quantity of instructions inserted into a composition. Was this a reaction to the Romantic ethos of freedom enjoyed by virtuosi in the nineteenth century? Certainly, nothing could be further from the spirit of a Liszt Hungarian Rhapsody than the painstaking detail notated in most of Bartók's solo piano works. Even a piece as deceptively simply as the little Bartók Sonatina is saturated with instructions, making it virtually impossible for a pianist without a photographic memory to reproduce everything exactly as requested. One wonders if a machine would be more successful for this purpose than a mere mortal...?! Yet the music itself is red-blooded, vibrant and emotionally charged.

How can one cope with this apparent contradiction? What scope for freedom if a performer's main energies have to be directed first – correctly – towards faithful reproduction of all the details? Before answering these questions, we need to consider how best to develop the ability to process and assimilate all the textual instructions presented on the printed score.

An exercise for developing textual fidelity

When attempting to clearly reproduce musical instructions on the printed page, it may be useful to write down on a blank sheet all the indications given about a particular phrase or section. The effectiveness of this practising method is that you are not distracted by the pitches of the music. You are able to focus on the patterns of phrase length and the dynamic hierarchy, as well as on the individual *staccato* markings, the accents, non-*legato* notes, and so on. It may be useful to divide up blank sheets into sections relating to lines of music, and to put in bar-lines in each line. Of course, this is rather academic, especially if you extend work in this area by closing your eyes and attempting to reiterate out loud from memory all the details you have just written down, but it can be an extremely effective method of working, even for the most elementary of piece. The example below shows how bars 26 (last beat) to 36 in the second movement of Beethoven's 'Moonlight' sonata might look when written down on plain paper:[48]

RH: Two 2-note slurs, one 4-note slur (last note *staccato*). Three further 2-note slurs, preceded by a single *staccato* note, one 3-note slur, one single non-*legato* note.

LH: Four *staccato* double notes, two 4-note slurs (last notes *staccato*), two non-*legato* notes, one 2-note slur, two non-*legato* notes.

Dynamics: *Piano. Cresecendo* from last beat of sixth bar to end of eighth bar. *Subito piano* for last two bars.

Using the 'wrong' dynamics in practice

In order to arrive at convincing dynamics in your repertoire, try playing each marked dynamic in a piece you are studying at four different levels (for example, at *pp*, *p*, *mf* and *f*).[49] This is similar to the approach taken to develop dynamic contrasts in Chapter 5 (p.47). Be as precise as you can with your dynamic differentiations in this useful exercise. When you return to playing the piece at the written dynamic levels, make sure that you are mentally relating the tone you produce at every moment to the three other dynamic levels you practised beforehand. The point is that your inner ear should be aware of sounds both louder and softer than the sounds you are producing at any one time. Mastering this approach in different parts of your repertoire will enable

---

48 NB shorthand according to personal taste is definitely worth experimenting with when 'practising' music like this!
49 This approach is similar to that adopted in Chapter 5, 'Colour', when it was suggested that a passage is repeated up to eight times in succession with a different dynamic level on each repetition.

you to have an awareness of a 'tonal hierarchy' in your inner ear. Eventually, it will make it possible for you to be able to produce a convincing range of dynamics that loyally follows the instructions from the composer in all of your performances.

Faithfully reproducing instructions from the composer that relate to pedalling, phrasing and articulation can be worked at in a different way. Begin working at a passage with mixed articulation (slurs and *staccatos*) by playing everything *legato*. You can then 'colour' the passage by gradually adding in all the articulation at a slow tempo – possibly hands separately at first – before attempting to play hands together. This same approach works well when attempting to pedal exactly as the composer has written. It is so much easier to 'add in' pedal from a bone-dry practice attempt with no involvement from the feet than to try to take pedalling away from a smudged, incoherent texture.

Aural photography

Clearly, interpretation must begin with a deep respect for the composer's written instructions. Without parameters for freedom, we are left in a huge vacuum. Lack of awareness of the text leads to a lack of focus, making the whole ritual of re-creative performance appear largely pointless. If we can achieve the equivalent of an 'aural photograph' by closely reproducing marks on the text as we play, there will unquestionably be more authenticity in our playing than if we wilfully ignore the composer's written instructions. In order to achieve mastery it is essential to be focused and concentrated on the task in hand. Merely 'reproducing' all of a composer's instructions on the text can be an extremely challenging task. As already mentioned, you need only look at one of the easier pieces by Bartók to see how detailed textual markings around notes can be! For pianists, cultivating an 'aural photograph' takes a considerable amount of effort and energy, and though it is a worthy endeavour, it should be practised with a caution. Aural photography can become prescriptive, literal and dry – almost uncreative. It is all too easy to lose sight of the bigger, emotionally charged picture when there are so many rules and regulations that need to be followed! This can lead to much frustration, especially if there is a conflict between what a student instinctively wants to do in a passage and what the composer requests on the printed page. How can one balance fidelity to the text with a need for inspiration and freedom? Is there a way to be simultaneously both reverential and creative? There is so much more to advanced interpretation than literal reproduction. But aural photography is vital as a first step. It is an essential prerequisite if you wish to achieve true integrity in performance.

The technique of freedom within discipline

'Music was born free, and to win freedom is its destiny.' Busoni's famous words may at first appear strange to those of us who regularly try to instil respect for instructions on the printed page into the playing of our students. Where does freedom fit with musical discipline? Clearly, the reproduction in sound of printed instructions is only the beginning of interpretation. As you become more confident, experienced and adventurous you will find that the challenge is not so much to show the difference between *forte* and *piano* as to find a way of capturing the particular quality of tone within the prescribed dynamic marking indicated. I am reminded of the words of the late Russian pedagogue Vera Gornostaeva, who was apparently fond of quoting George Bernard Shaw's saying 'There are fifty ways of saying "yes" and five hundred ways of saying "no", but only one way of writing them down.'[50] This approach can be extended to rhythmic freedom as well as touch. With regard to the latter, we commented in Chapter 3 on the infinite range of tonal variety that can be explored on the piano. The same is true in terms of articulation: 'staccato', for example, is generally considered an indication of 'detached' playing, but clearly many different types of *staccato* are possible on a modern grand piano, and it is up to the pianist to decide just how short or long an individual *staccato* marking should be played. Again, there is no reason for the exclusion of beginners and elementary players here: they should be able to cope with different approaches to articulation within the stipulated markings on the printed text.

But of course, it is impossible (and indeed undesirable) to notate all the variations in dynamics, rhythm and articulation that are possible when interpreting the limited number of markings even the most painstakingly detailed composer may notate. When considering the quality of particular markings on the text, experimentation at the piano is vital, with your ears acting as judge and jury over decisions about how long/short, sharp/mellow or soft/loud particular *staccatos*, accents, *mezzo staccatos* or *sforzandos* should be.

Stylistic techniques

How do we make our performances of Bach sound like Bach? What is it that differentiates Bach-playing from Mozart-playing? The whole issue of how to faithfully, sensitively and idiomatically interpret the music we study is often shrouded in mystery and uncertainty for younger players, but a few basic points related to textual fidelity and freedom within it can now be made which should enable stylistic study to proceed with greater clarity and awareness.

Steep yourself in music!

Musical taste, knowledge and experience play an enormous part in developing an awareness of style. In order to have the confidence and conviction to be able to interpret markings on the text, it is vital that you steep yourself in as much music as possible. We are not just talking about other piano pieces by Beethoven here as a means of improving your performance of one piece by that composer. If you want to understand the style of Beethoven's celebrated Op.33 Bagatelles, for example, then it makes sense to listen to his first two symphonies, six Op.18

50 Sergei Babayan in interview, quoted by Norman Lebrecht on the website *Slipped Disc*. www.slippedisc.com

quartets and possibly also the Op.31 sonatas as well. This reservoir of repertoire will provide you with a sense of perspective when it comes to finding the range of possibilities for balancing chords, pedalling, choosing tempos, and so on in the Bagatelles. Moreover, it will be a joy to broaden your listening range and discover masterpieces previously unheard by your ears.

Certainly, there is a wide range of written material that can help enormously when it comes to interpretation. Thanks to the internet it is remarkably easy to hear performances of Baroque and Classical music on harpsichords and fortepianos. Historical perspective and general knowledge of the instruments used in the time of Bach, Mozart and Chopin will do no harm at all for pianists to explore – even when they are working at the earliest stages and preliminary grades. Of course, there are many possibilities for interpretation, and here is not the place to be a law giver with regard to how you add ornaments in Bach's 'Anna Magdalena' notebook; whether or not you use pedal in early Haydn sonatas; or what speed you should adopt for Beethoven's 'Moonlight' sonata. A quick survey of performances of the 'Moonlight' from half a dozen great pianists on disc will quickly reveal huge differences in approach. As is so often the case in musical interpretation, it is not so much what you do as how you do it. Conviction over interpretive issues will come if you are able to sing, dance, breathe, conduct or speak the phrases you are playing. In Baroque and Classical music in particular, it can help to imagine how the music you are playing on the keyboard would sound if it were performed by instrumentalists. In virtually all periods, it will be helpful to imagine your melodic lines sung. Let's go back to the opening of Schumann's 'First Loss' (see p.76):

The piece clearly belongs in the Romantic stylistic period, but it could be made to sound Baroque if the left-hand part is projected on an equal footing to the right. This would turn the music into something close in style to a Bach Two-Part Invention! Clearly, Schumann had a songlike quality in mind here, so it would be stylistically appropriate to use a little pedal on the longer melodic notes, capturing some added resonance to the chords that these notes form with the left hand. Care has to be taken in interpreting the accent markings on the upbeat quavers at the start of each phrase – if these are interpreted literally, then a pseudo-twentieth-century syncopated attack would result, turning the music into something similar to Prokofiev or even Bartók.

Continuing the compositional process

Of course, some works in the repertoire have fewer written requests on the musical text from the composer than others. This is especially true in repertoire from the pre-Beethoven era. When there is a lack of information from the composer, it is the interpreter's duty to continue where the composer left off. This can be done by adding ornamentation and colouring as well as by projecting subjective, personal ideas onto notes on the score. These can, indeed should, be related to touch, sound, voicing, pedalling, rhythm, *rubato* and phrasing. In many ways the performer becomes a composer too when involved in studying the music of Bach, Haydn and Mozart, to name but a few composers of relevance in this context. Because improvisation was much more of an essential technical tool in a musician's armoury in the eighteenth century than it is today, and because music was less of a personalised art in the age of musical patronage than it became later, the text was considered only the beginning of a performance. The examples below show the openings of the Allemande and Gigue movements from Bach's Partita No.6 in E minor:

Both movements demand considerable subjective input from the performer: in the Allemande there are all sorts of possibilities that can be adopted in terms of ornamentation. The melodic line can easily take appoggiaturas, whilst phrasing in the manner of a cellist's bowing may seem appropriate for the articulation of the left hand. The Gigue is highly controversial, as it is possible to completely re-write the time signature and realise the music in compound time! Performers these days are equally divided over whether to do this or not. Whatever the performer's choice, decisions also need to be made with regard to articulation, dynamics, fingering and tempo – all of which can be considered as a continuation of composition.

And exactly the same is true for music written after 1800! Real fidelity to the text allows for maximum freedom of expression from the performer. This crucial fact is often overlooked by inexperienced teachers, who often feel that remaining loyal to the written instructions on the text is enough. It is not! We have already mentioned that music notation is extremely limited and approximate. But the magic and creativity comes from refining and choosing from the infinite range of shades possible within the parameters laid down. This is where real freedom resides – in small, carefully considered and measured differences of approach. We should never underestimate just how much freedom we actually possess as interpreters, especially when we observe every printed marking to the letter in a Beethoven sonata, Bartók Romanian dance or Debussy étude.

16 Fingering

The Basics

Perhaps nothing is more important for sustained technical success in performance than reliable and effective fingering. The art of fingering is a voluminous subject but we can usefully instil ideas and approaches that can be built on and expanded by individual players over a sustained period. In order to begin making progress, let us identify six essential principles:

Six basic rules of fingering

1 Revise your scale fingerings.
2 Always know where your thumbs should be.
3 Find and repeat finger patterns.
4 Never over complicate.
5 Use symmetry as much as possible.
6 Fingering is never generic.

---

1. Revise your scale fingerings. Use your scale fingerings as a reference point. Scales are extremely important for all kinds of reasons. However, their necessity for an understanding of how fingering works is a prime reason for their mastery. The earliest stages of learning a piece must include lots of work on fingering. This is true for pianists of every level and ability.

Clearly, the catalogue of all basic scale patterns must be fully assimilated in order to finger music with authority. Most of the standard repertoire we play is built from scale patterns and it therefore follows that an infallible security over scale fingerings is essential. Begin fingering a new piece by relating passages in it to basic scale and arpeggio fingerings. By doing this, you are empowering your facility and relating all the hours of practice you have already done on fingering scales and arpeggios to music, rather than just to the technical section of an exam syllabus. Never forget that 99% of pieces are scales and arpeggios in disguise! I recommend purchasing either the ABRSM manual of scales and arpeggios[51] or Trinity Guildhall's comparable volume.[52] Both publications contain excellent fingerings for all major and minor scales and arpeggios.

The passage below comes from Clementi (bars 54–8 of the Sonatina in C, Op.36 No.1, third movement) and shows in the simplest terms how technical security can be immediately encouraged through fingering based on the standard simple scale and arpeggio patterns we learn from Grade 1 upwards.

---

51 The Manual of Scales, Broken Chords and Arpeggios, ed. Ruth Gerald (ABRSM Publishing, 2006).
52 Trinity Guildhall *Piano Scales and Arpeggios Initial–Grade 5* (2006) and *Piano Scales and Arperggios Grade 6–8* (2006).

Thus the right hand in this passage becomes simple to practise when the thumb is placed on all the Fs and Cs – just as one does in the C major scale. It is not necessary to pencil in any other fingering in this passage, as awareness of where the thumbs are placed will automatically position the other fingers over all the other notes. The same is true of the left hand. Here it is advisable for technical security to literally cover the notes of every bar in advance so that the fingers 'touch and press' the notes rather than strike them from above. Covering notes in advance makes memorising easier. It also ensures more technical security and encourages beautiful sound production.

2 Always know where your thumbs should be. As touched on above, fingering in most passages is dictated by where the thumbs go. Too often students become frustrated and perplexed by attempting to write into their copies every single fingering, and it is often a complete waste of time to write in other fingerings as it crowds the page. Write in '1' wherever you feel the thumb should play. Provided you know your scale fingerings, if you know where your thumbs are going, then all the other fingers should slot into place easily (although it can be useful to write in whether the third or fourth finger should be used). By simply notating each thumb move, it is possible to quickly grasp position changes and thus immediately have a technical bird's-eye view of a whole movement. It is also vital to work out where the thumbs go in both hands. Too often fingerings that work well hands separately become over-complicated or clumsy when put together.

3. Find and repeat finger patterns. Find patterns/sequences in your fingering and stick to them. Good fingering is usually simple, easy to remember and compatible with the phrasing and musical character of the piece. It therefore follows that it is much easier to memorise a piece in which you use repetitive finger patterns than if you change the approach to fingering throughout. It is far easier to find sequences of finger patterns in non-*legato* and *staccato* passages than in *legato* passages. 'Overlapping' or 'physical' *legato* at the piano (see *The Foundations of Technique*, p.38) is something that takes years to develop. Fingering is a vital aspect of this, and without extremely refined and skilful coordination, beautiful *legato* (and the exquisite *cantabile* that results) is simply not possible. However, *staccato* and non-*legato* phrases can be fingered simply, logically and consistently in chordal 'blocks' or 'boxes' with the arm moving the hand from one group of notes to another. Practise by telescoping each block/box into a 'chordal bunch' of notes. There are many examples of this in all stylistic periods from grade 4 repertoire upwards, but let's look at the first movement of Beethoven's 'Emperor' Piano Concerto No.5 Op.73 (bars 292–4). Fingering unfolds clearly in 'blocks' corresponding to each half-bar segment:

4. Do not over complicate! There is nothing worse than trying to assimilate fingering that uses too many changes of position (i.e. too many thumbs) and which therefore requires many pencil markings on the score. Simplicity in fingering can be shown by writing squares or circles around each group of notes on the page. If this is hard to do, the chances are that the fingering is too difficult to assimilate and will therefore always feel awkward.

5. Use symmetry as much as possible. Principles of symmetry are helpful in fingering at the keyboard, and for that reason I always stress the importance of working at contrary-motion scales as a means of building up basic expertise. When writing in fingering for one hand, remember that we play with two hands, and fingering that can work very well when you are practising hands separately can be disastrous when you start working hands together. When faced with busy passages that use semiquavers in each hand, it is good to make sure that the thumbs play in each hand at the same time, and to relate fingering as much as possible to that for contrary-motion scales.

6. Fingering is never generic. Though fingering on the printed page of a reputable edition may be a good starting point for study, it is important to remember that every individual player is different. You cannot clone fingering so that one choice of options is used by everyone on the planet. Of course, hand size plays an enormous part in the choice of fingering. Small hands will inevitably find that certain passages prove impossible to execute, and in such contexts careful decisions over the omission of notes need to be made. 'Faking it' is a highly skilful art, dependant on sensitive tonal balancing, timing and lateral thinking. This leads naturally on to an even broader consideration of 'arrangements between the hands'. Clearly, this controversial subject can bring on apoplexy amongst the purists. At its most distasteful and ludicrous, I immediately think of an approach to the opening of Chopin's Étude Op.25 No.6, wherein the thirds, written exclusively for the right hand, are played by both hands! Clearly, this is simply unacceptable, for it takes away from the character and *raison d'être* of the study. However, other 'arrangements' can be extremely beneficial, and it is wrong to be overly puritanical here. No listener will object to an 'easy' two-hand solution to a technical problem if the performer is talented enough to adopt the approach in a musical way. This means that careful practice is needed so that the technical 'trick' remains aurally invisible.

A sound principle to follow is that arrangements and omissions of notes are perfectly acceptable – provided that the listener is unaware of what the performer is doing. In fingering and re-arranging at the keyboard, nothing is sinful unless it is aurally detectible!

Further principles and approaches

Finger substitution

On an immediately practical level, pianists can learn significant skills from organists. 'Finger substitution' is a rudimentary skill on the organ, and on the piano it can be used wherever a totally watertight join is necessary in order to achieve the richest possible *legato* on the instrument. This can be seen in the late Romantic repertoire in particular, and Brahms' Intermezzo in A, Op.118 No.2), presents a classic case. Students are often surprised when fingerings such as those in this example are used to ensure a truly idiomatic depth of sound throughout a phrase:

Clearly, it is vital for the player to relax arms and wrists completely behind the (strong) bridge of the hand in contexts such as this.

When using finger substitution it is also very important to remember that we do not normally play 'mono-linear' music, and that the contrapuntal diversity of our music can often be enhanced by opting to choose finger substitution in one part and non-*legato* in the others. The example below – the D minor fugue from Book 2 of *The Well-Tempered Clavier* – shows how the soprano part of the fugue plays *legato*, whilst the lower alto part in the same hand could opt for non-*legato*. Of course, this mix of finger substitution with non-*legato* or *staccato* fingering can be extended to chordal playing too, especially if there is a need to bring out a melody line across chordal progressions.

'The sixth finger'

In bravura repertoire, where élan and temperamental flourish is part of the attraction, using what Busoni called 'the sixth finger' may be appropriate. This is a somewhat tongue-in-cheek nickname for slide fingering, and it can be extremely useful for those contexts when you wish to imitate a Paganiniesque violin *glissando*, or simply for those moments when it is important not to get too deliberate and heavily accented in terms of tone. One immediately thinks of the way in which some of the chromatic scale runs in Liszt's transcendental études can be facilitated clearly via the use of sliding (see the chromatic-sixth ascending runs in 'Mazeppa', for instance), though even in Bach fugues it is often appropriate to slide on the thumb if it is in a lower part.[53] Such an approach can at times achieve much more *legato* than any other fingering.

Less use of the thumb leads to greater fluency

As mentioned in Chapter 10 ('Speed'), the general rule is that you will be able to play much faster if you use fewer thumb shifts than if you use more. It is fascinating to study fingerings in the scale exercises of both Cortot's *Rational Principles of Technique* and Busoni's *Klavierübung*. Each author advocates practising scale patterns with unorthodox fingerings such as 1-2-3-1-2-3 and even 1-2-3-4-5-1-2-3-4-5, etc. Fingerings like these should be extended in interpretation so that the pianist has a wide range of possibilities. Certainly, in practice the scale fingering that appears to be the most characterful for the passage in question should be the fingering that is adopted.

Tonal balancing and fingering

Of course, fingering can enhance chordal balancing tremendously. So often pianists innocently use the fifth finger for low solitary notes when the biggest sonority possible is required. In such contexts it is often far more impressive to use the thumb, even if it means that a high level of elbow/arm flexibility is required in order to manoeuvre around the keyboard. Similarly, I often use the thumb on right-hand notes at the top of the keyboard, and the athletic 'madness' that regularly results in order to achieve this fingering can be exciting and exhilarating, as well as extremely risky (remember Schnabel's famous quote 'safety last!' in this context).

Fingering as a creative means of expression

Though fingering is one of the first things to work on when preparing a new piece, it is one of the last things too. By that, I mean that the process of revision and reconsideration in fingering is endless, and constantly bewildering. Of course, it is foolhardy for inexperienced players in particular to change fingerings too close to a concert performance. It is probably not such a bright idea for professional pianists to adopt either! However, it would be artistically stifling to feel that one had ever found the 'ultimate answers' to every fingering in a great masterpiece. Indeed, many concert pianists express amazement

---

53 See slide fingering for chromatic double-third scales in *The Foundations of Technique*, p77.

at the fact that when they return to 'old' repertoire, fingerings that were previously adopted seem to be unpractical and need to be changed!

Quite clearly, fingering is a very personal thing, dependant not only on hand size but also on taste and artistic preference. Fingering should be thought of as an inspiring, creative art rather than as a dull chore. Debussy emphasised this in the introduction to his (famously unfingered) *Études*, where he called on pianists to 'search' for their own fingerings in the music rather than conform to the suggestions of others. In addition, how wonderfully liberated and stimulating a 'fingerless' page of Debussy's music is when compared to the tyrannical demands written into copies not only by non-negotiable teachers but also by inflexible editors, even in highly respected 'urtext' publications.

The personalities of each finger

By avoiding the use of the thumb on upbeats, first notes of phrases, offbeats and weak beats/parts of beats, phrases can become less percussive and more poetically charged. Of course, one has to develop the skills to 'hide' accents generated by the thumbs, but nonetheless it is important to exploit the natural qualities of each finger; in the case of the thumb, this means reserving its use for emphasis at strong moments in the music in particular, as well as using it as a technical 'anchor', a pivotal force, in virtually every phrase. It is interesting to see how strong the third finger is too. Quite often trills executed with 1 and 3 are more declamatory and strong than when 1 is used with 2. Of course, the fourth finger is especially suited to veiled and *leggiero* contexts – scale runs can immediately entice!

The closing section of the slow movement in the Brahms D minor Concerto can attain ethereal spirituality and luminescence by the use of the weakest fingers in both the trills and the demisemiquaver flourishes. In unique contexts such as this, special solutions need to be strived for in order to arrive at the most inspirational and beautiful digital patterns. Tactile artistry remains one of the greatest challenges in piano playing, but also one of the most rewarding aspects of practice.

Phrasing and style

Once the logic and essential principles of fingering are understood, progress is achieved for the most part via stylistic and musical sensitivity. When time and effort has been spent training the 'weaker' fingers not to be afraid, a whole gamut of possibilities opens up. In terms of phrasing and pianistic oratory, finger choices have a huge and under-appreciated role to play. A good example of this can be found in the soloist's first entry in Beethoven's C minor Concerto: the use of the thumb at the top of each pianistic flourish can immediately establish extrovert drama and excitement in a way in which conventional fingering (i.e. using the fifth finger instead of the thumb before the rests) cannot. The excerpt below is taken from Beethoven's 'Appassionata' sonata, first movement. By fingering all of the arpeggios in one hand, tremendous excitement and energy are maintained. If the pianist divides this passage between the hands, much of the characterisation is lost.

We should learn not to restrict our choices to those that are most convenient or comfortable. Try to aim for a constant curiosity so that a quest for alternative solutions and ideas is never lost. In repeated notes, for example, it may not always be musically desirable to use more than one finger! And in soaring *legato* lines, I personally am loathe to break up the musical flow by dividing up sections between the hands – in the famous opening arpeggios of Chopin's *Polonaise-Fantaisie*, I use the left hand throughout. On the other hand, when energised volatility is required, nothing quite beats the physical exuberance of dividing up rapid-fire passagework between the left and right hands. So much depends on the effect desired, though obviously there has to be consistency: once you begin to shape a fugue subject via a particular fingering, you must continue to use the same fingering throughout the remainder of the fugue in order to achieve a logical approach to the piece as a whole.

Fingering is more of an art than a technical accomplishment, though we can learn much from the basic technical skills necessary to play other instruments. One could discuss at length, for example, the similarities between fingering choices for pianists, bowing for string players and breathing for wind instrumentalists.

For maverick eccentricity in the name of characterisation, try the crazy thumbs approach shown in the last movement of Beethoven's Op.10 No.2 Sonata (bars 76–84):

More elegance and organic connection with the keyboard is apparent in the specialised approach suggested by the fingering shown here for Chopin (F major Prelude, Op.28 No.23):

Though this is clearly only for those with large hands and highly developed elasticity, it does show how smoothness and grace can arise by placing the thumb in the middle, pivotal region of an arpeggiated flourish rather than over the bottom note(s).

Countless other examples could be quoted here in a subject worth at least one hefty volume. There are moments when you may wish to project impassioned outbursts by using the thumb alone (e.g. every single one of the left-hand notes in bars 18–19 of the slow movement of Beethoven's 'Les Adieux' sonata Op.81a) and other moments when you may wish to avoid the thumb completely, lest it ruin the seamless grace and elegance of the melodic line (for example, in the right-hand opening line of Mozart's A major Sonata, K.331, first movement).

17 Practising

Mastering the art of practising can prove challenging. This is hardly surprising, as successful practising requires many skills. Excellent practising needs strong focus, the ability to listen both sensitively and objectively, patience, will power, a serene outlook and strong organisation. It is asking an awful lot of young inexperienced pianists in particular to expect them to practise on their own for extended periods of time each day. Indeed, there are many written accounts of how child prodigies over the centuries often benefitted by having hours of daily 'supervised practice': devoted parents would take up a seated position on a regular basis next to the piano in order to ensure that their young son or daughter remained constantly focused on improving their piano playing.[54]

Since its launch by Shinichi Suzuki in the 1950s, the 'Suzuki method' of teaching has shown how excellent practice can be developed from the earliest stages via strong organisation, imitation of others and parental involvement. Children are encouraged to observe the music lessons of elder siblings or more senior students before beginning their own formal lessons. They gradually acclimatise to a musical environment and have constant support as they journey towards mastery of their chosen instrument. The approach to learning is seen not as an exclusively singular vocation for the child, but as an activity in which the whole family at home can be involved.

However, in our fast-moving, stress-ridden twenty-first century world, supervised practice may not be a feasible option on a regular basis for many parents. In any case, it is not an option for adult learners. How can inexperienced players learn to improve their practising techniques? It has to be said that even if supervised practice were a real possibility, ultimately the goal in this area – as in all areas of piano technique – should be independence. Pianists need to learn to work confidently and effectively on their own. Let us consider how this ideal can become a reality.

Plan–Play–Review in bite-size segments

The threefold self-listening practice routine of work outlined in Chapter 1 should always be remembered in practice sessions: begin with an inner conception. Continue by playing a small segment of music aloud. Finish with an objective self-review and evaluation of what you have done. Repeat this process. Indeed, Plan–Play–Review, or PPR for short, should be repeated for a single passage as often as is necessary for you to feel that results have been achieved. Always ask questions: What am I trying to do? What are the best ways of working to get what I want? Should I try a different approach? Remember that repetition with no mistakes is an absolute necessity. If you practise mistakes, you will perform mistakes! Slow repetition of PPR using

---

54 In Edward Dent's 1935 biography *Ferruccio Busoni* (Eulenberg), p.156, there is a vivid description of the supervised practice Busoni received as a young child from his tyrannical father.

the smallest sections (often only a bar or a segment from a bar) can be an extremely effective and efficient method of assimilating, perfecting and securing permanently a new fingering or position of the hands, or of simply of memorising a difficult corner.[55] Above all, listen! As mentioned in Chapter 1, your ears are your best tutor, and you must develop the ability to listen critically to your own practice as you play. As you repeat a particular passage, your ears will guide you over balancing, phrasing, pedalling and colouring.

Notebooks and diaries

If all of this proves rather challenging, it may be useful to keep a record of what you have done each day in a written diary. This can be fascinating to read over for self-review purposes. It is also helpful to plan in advance by writing down what you hope to achieve. Try writing down a mini plan for all your practice sessions in one day. Be as specific and detailed as possible. You could, for instance, divide the day into exercises first (five minutes), then go on to fifteen minutes of scales, five minutes of concentrated sight-reading, then fifteen minutes on your study. This gets the 'nuts and bolts' aspect of your piano work out of the way in one forty-minute session of practice. Perhaps you are changing technique? If so, it can help to review what you are doing at regular intervals during practice sessions by taking time to specifically observe and note your personal posture, hand positions, and so on. You may find it useful to have a personalised warm-up and cooling-down routine. Remember also that you should not launch straight into the loudest and fastest of pieces at the beginning of a practice session. In addition, whilst you practise it can be physically and mentally very helpful simply to walk round the room for a little while: taking mini breaks of up to thirty seconds can make a huge difference to your attitude and focus.

In planning, it may be helpful to schedule repertoire for later practice sessions in the day. If you choose to work on two short pieces in a single forty-minute session, be very clear in your own mind over what it is you are going to do. Do not just start playing through the piece vaguely, hoping for the best. If you must 'play through' the piece in its entirety, make sure that you do so very slowly in the early stages, following every detail, and getting the fingering accurate.

In a practice diary, it can sometimes be most helpful to write down as many different ways as you can think of to practice a particular movement. You could divide the piece into sections and think of alternative ways to work on particular passages. By consistently expanding the horizons of your knowledge in this way, and by opening your mind at the planning, pre-practice stage to some of the endless possibilities, your practising should remain vibrantly inspired and energised.

---

55   However, do bear in mind that memorising can be separated from work on improving the *quality* of the way you play a particular piece. We will look at memorising techniques in the next chapter.

Focus, consistency and health

The art of practising takes years to develop.[56] Indeed, practising should
be considered a journey without end; a ceaseless quest for creativity and
inspiration. Clearly, it is important to begin and remain focused when you
are working in a practice room. Take time to set yourself up comfortably at
the instrument and to ensure that your mind does not wander. Any form of
physical discomfort whilst playing is bad news, so always take time to listen
to your body. Combining an effortless ease of approach with attentive ears, a
determined spirit and lively intellectual curiosity is the ideal. Always be aware
of what you are doing. Never be vague over fingering. Once a fingering has been
written into the copy or a printed fingering suggestion has been approved,
stick with it. Of course, you can make changes to fingering (or indeed anything
else) at any stage of the practising process, but it is important to change things
consciously rather than carelessly. Practising should be an opportunity to aim
for perfection. If you can produce blemish-free pianism in a slow tempo during
your practice hours then you will be nourishing a wonderful sense of security
and a greater awareness of what you are trying to achieve.

As has already been mentioned, concentration and self-listening skills are vital.
During practice sessions, it is much easier to remain 'on message' and attentive
to the task in hand if your ears are wide open and receptive to the quality of
sound you are producing at all times. Never play without an awareness of the
quality of tone you are producing. This is as true for slow-tempo practising as
for every other activity at the instrument. Clearly, practising will be even more
successful if you are physically in good shape. It helps if you can maintain a
balanced lifestyle with a balanced diet, plenty of sleep, lots of fresh air and
exercise. Taking time out for recreation will make your concentration and
determination to succeed much stronger when you do practise.

Micro-practising

Keyboard players probably deal with more notes per bar than string or wind
players. Because of this, it can be all too easy for them to feel overwhelmed
when it comes to practising. 'Too many notes and too little time' is a frequent
problem that amateur pianists in particular tend to complain about, though it
would be wrong to say that professional pianists never feel the same way! It is
therefore important to concentrate efforts and focus on the specific problem
areas in your repertoire that cause you difficulties. Stephen Hough[57] and others
have shown in their writings that it is often two linking notes, or a single shift
of position, that causes anxiety and stress in repertoire. If you can identify
the jump or two-note link that is causing angst in a problematic passage,

56 Indeed, a full and exhaustive study of practising is beyond the scope of this book. In addition
to the already mentioned *Practising the Piano* by Frank Merrick, recommended books for further
study include *The Art of Practising: A guide to making music from the heart*, by Madeline Bruser (1999);
Successful Practising: A handbook for pupils, parents and music teachers, by Jenny Macmillan (2010); and
Practiceopedia: The music student's illustrated guide to practising, by Philip Johnston (2007). There is also
an extensive series of Kindle edition books available by Graham Fitch, entitled *Practising the Piano*.
57 Stephen Hough blog for Daily Telegraph: http://blogs.telegraph.co.uk/culture/author/stephenhough/

difficulties can be swiftly overcome. By working on the linking jumps between position changes in a challenging passage, it is possible to save lots of time and also really understand and overcome the difficulties that are preventing you from playing with total command. This means that instead of playing through difficult pages or phrases endlessly, you end up practising pairs of notes from the problem section, working hard to move from one part of the keyboard to another with coordination, economy of movement and a sense of control. Let's call this approach to work 'micro-practising'. 'Good practising means that listeners are unable to tell which piece is being practised' comes to mind in this context, and I am grateful to Philip Fowke for instilling this concept in a memorable class he gave many years back in Manchester.[58] The late Shura Cherkassky's approach is also worth holding up as an excellent example: there was one memorable occasion when the great pianist was due to perform in Glasgow and spent an earlier part of the day in the hall working in concentrated bundles of notes at the keyboard. There were many 'silent' moves too over the keyboard (so-called 'shadow' practice). One was left with the impression that there was not a single second of practising done by Cherkassky that was wasted. His example of concentration and microscopic precision shows us all the importance of conserving energy and tuning directly into issues that need to be resolved.

These examples highlight the position changes that occur in the C major scale and arpeggio:

Of course, every pianist from Grade 1 onwards is aware of these! However, what many players forget is that it is really only the highlighted position changes that present difficulties in the scale and arpeggio. Why waste time playing through all the notes endlessly when time would be more profitably spent concentrating on secure coordination over the position-change notes? It could well be argued that added security will most effectively come from isolating the position changes and working on them via transposition into all the different keys. In this way you are giving yourself slight variations in the technical difficulty and also bringing systematic order to your practising, so that when similar position shifts occur in different keys, they will not prove challenging.

Let's now look at some examples from the concert repertoire in which the isolation of position changes/groups of 2–3 notes is essential for progress.

1 This excerpt comes from the first phrase in one of the most notoriously challenging octave sections of Tchaikovsky's first piano concerto.

58 Masterclass at Chetham's School of Music, 2007.

Students often sweat endlessly over this section of the work, becoming more tense, hot and flustered as a result, and often failing to feel more comfortable with its demands. However, when you analyse the section it quickly becomes evident that the real difficulty in execution lies in negotiating the pairs of octave leaps that occur within the torrent of notes. As in scale and arpeggio position changes, this issue is best tackled by isolating the problem. Work on the pairs of leaps on their own. It is useful to practise quick 'trigger' movements and to vary the dynamics. You will get less tired and have more energy if you work quietly. Try a light, *leggiero* touch at first, then gradually increase the depth of sound you are producing until you are playing each jump with full arm weight, triple *fortissimo*. It is also a good idea to repeat this process through the entire spectrum of dynamics with your eyes shut, then to do all of this with each pair from the passage transposed into all keys (for the same reasons that transposition of position shifts in scales and arpeggios is recommended above). Another approach to the problem would be to do trigger-movement practice on each leap but to land silently on the second octave in each pair of notes. You can also try jumping onto the second octave in each pair, beginning with a silent first octave in each case!

2 The second example is from Book 1 of Brahms' 'Paganini' Variations and frequently causes frustration amongst students, not least because double sixths – a rather specialised pianistic phenomenon – can appear daunting on the page:

However, there is hope, and the 'cure' for anxiety here is similar to that found in the Tchaikovsky concerto. By isolating the position shifts and playing the three-note manoeuvre in each change of position, it is possible to focus immediately on the problem. It is also good with double notes to try playing just the top notes (but keeping the fingering the same as when you play the lower notes too), then just the lower notes. Personally, I find it saves energy to begin working on double-note manoeuvres such as these by practising the notes silently on the keys – 'shadowing' the notes rather than depressing them. This is also a good method of work in that it encourages you to look more closely at how your fingers are moving (without the distraction of sound!). Keep your fingers as close as possible to the keys and refrain from any unnecessary extra movements. The highlighted jumps require the utmost concentration of movement and should ideally be played with a 'touch and press' approach (whereby the fingers are on the key surface before the notes are played). In this way it is much easier to synchronise and coordinate the playing of both hands.

3 In the final example ('Children Quarrelling at Play', from Mussorgsky's *Pictures at an Exhibition*), the pianistic awkwardness in negotiating so many semiquavers in such short spaces of time can appear frustrating.

It is worth extending the principle of practising suggested for the Brahms and Tchaikovsky a little here, and trying to play the whole passage in pairs of semiquavers, pair by pair. Work on each manoeuvre from semiquaver to semiquaver – in isolation, so you can check that your fingers are behaving themselves as they move through each quarter of each beat. Try silent practice on the key surface first, then quick movements from the first to second semiquavers, then second to third, third to fourth, and so on. As in the Brahms example, it may be helpful to play the top line of notes on their own first (again, using the fingering you will use when playing all the notes). As the challenge here is to aim for a lighter touch whilst retaining clarity, it may be helpful first to master the passage *fortissimo*, then to gradually lighten the articulation and dynamic level until you can cope easily with the requisite *leggiero* touch.

Theodor Leschetizky

The pianist–composer Theodor Leschetizky (1830–1915) is a legendary figure in the history of piano pedagogy. Though born before the death of Chopin, he lived beyond the birth of Shostakovich, so his lifetime was marked by astonishing musical and historical changes. Leschetizky was taught by Czerny and counted Brahms, Liszt and Anton Rubinstein amongst his friends.[59] We can still learn much from his example and influence today, as there is much material available for study via the writings of his students and disciples. Indeed, Leschetizky's assistants collated a number of his exercises together (some of which are still available in a modern revised edition[60]) to form what has become branded and widely renowned as 'the Leschetizky method'. This 'method' became legendary, despite the fact that the great man himself felt, according to his biographer Annette Hullah, that he never really used any 'method' as such as a teacher! Though Hullah's book[61] has long been out of print and may appear, to a modern reader, rather sentimental and approximate in terms of historical accuracy, it remains inspirational. In particular, its description of Lechetizky's insistence of small steps and clear thinking in practice – evidently a central element in his pedagogical approach – can teach us much about the art of practising today.

Let's examine and explore the *raison d'être* of Leschetizky's pedagogy as outlined (and indeed quoted) in Hullah's book. She mentions Leschetizky's insistence on clarity of thought in the music students are attempting to play, as well as an awareness of the challenges involved and a mental awareness of how these challenges are to be conquered before the notes are even played aloud. Hullah quotes the master directly to emphasise the vital guidelines that were essential in his pedagogical philosophy:

> Decide exactly what it is you want to do in the first place, and then how you will do it; then play it. Stop and think if you played it in the way you meant to do; then only, if sure of this, go ahead. Without concentration, remember, you can do nothing, the brain must guide the fingers, not the fingers the brain.

This in essence is a surefire method for extremely effective practising at all levels and in virtually all contexts. Of course, it goes without saying that for this approach to succeed, a pianist needs to have excellent self-listening skills, as well as objective, calm and reasoned reactions. The ability to be an effective self-critic in practice is vital if a pianist is to learn independence and so be able to cope without the need of a teacher during the hours of practice. It is something that can be developed gradually through encouragement and guidance in the teaching studio.

The Leschetizky approach works extremely well when used for micro-chunks of music rather than for large sections. Indeed, Hullah mentions the emphasis on practice in small sections earlier in her book, showing that Leschetizky was insistent on instilling a sense of perfection in all his students when working at music with them. This meant that every detail was internalised – 'heard' with the inner ear and 'seen' as a picture away from the piano. Hullah writes as follows:

---

59 As the teacher of Anna Yesipova, Richard Buhlig, Ignaz Friedman, Ignacy Jan Paderewski, Artur Schnabel, Mark Hambourg, Alexander Brailowsky, Alexander Winkler, Benno Moiseiwitsch, Mieczylaw Horszowski, Frank Merrick, Paul Wittgenstein and Natalia Polnazkovski (amongst scores of other excellent pianists), Leschetizky's influence was exceptional, leading many to declare him the greatest piano teacher of all time.
60 *The Leschetizky Method: A guide to fine and correct playing*, Malwine Brée, Seymour Bernstein (Courier Corporation, 1997).
61 Annette Hullah: *Theodor Leschetizky*. London Lane, 1906 (reprinted 1923).

He takes the first bar, or phrase … and dissects it until every marking is clear … he practises each detail as he comes to it. He puts all the parts together, learning it by heart as he goes, finishing one section, making it as perfect as he can in every respect, both technically and musically, before he attempts the next. What is required of him is that he shall study every piece of music so thoroughly that he knows every detail of it, can play any part of it accurately, beginning at any point, and that he can visualise the whole without the music – that is, see in his mind what is written, without either notes or instrument.

How far removed is this approach from the impatience and time wasting so often seen with many students! How sad that precious hours are thrown away through mindless repetitions of passages over and over again. Such an approach is always doomed to failure – yet it is still one of the most common tendencies worldwide.

Students certainly need to be patient when following Leschetizky's approach, but the results for those that persevere will unquestionably be satisfying. In addition, it is interesting to note that Leschetizky, like Chopin before him, was not in favour of students practising regularly for more than three hours per day. Intensive productivity in manageable chunks of work seems to have been his preferred and recommended system of working. Hullah emphasises

---

Summary for effective practising

- Always ask questions: What am I trying to do? What are the best ways of working to get what I want? Should I try a different approach?
- Keep a practice diary for planning and reviewing daily work.
- Remember that slow work with no mistakes is essential.
- Repetition in small sections (often of only a bar or even part of a bar) can be the most effective way of learning and memorising music.
- Be consistent with fingering as you repeat passages whilst practising.
- Listen, listen and listen again!
- You should never feel discomfort as you play. Think at regular intervals during the practice session about posture, hand positions, etc.
- Warming-up and cooling-down should be part of daily practising, as should mini breaks, which should be scheduled sensibly.
- Keep fit and healthy, and get lots of sleep. Eat well and enjoy recreation. These things are basic and will largely determine how successful your work is.
- In general, avoid merely playing through your repertoire.
- Do not allow errors to pass – go back immediately and correct mistakes.
- Aim for a quality of sound in keeping with a firm, secure grasp of the notes – do not be sketchy and vague in your approach.

this further in her book with the fascinating suggestion that 'any one with the power of concentration can learn to play by heart'. Leschetizky expected every student to study 'bar by bar, slowly and deliberately engraving each point on his mind as in a map'. He is quoted as saying that 'one page a day so learnt will give you a trunkful of music or your repertoire at the end of the year'. How many students have the patience to consistently devote a whole day to only one page of music at a time? Never was the old fable of the hare and the tortoise more apposite!

Further thoughts on practising: 'the practice list'

A few years ago, in tongue-in-cheek mode, I casually suggested to all my students that what piano teachers really needed for an easy life was a list of all possible practice methods. Teaching thereafter would be a simple procedure whereby after a student lesson performance, the teacher could say something like 'thank you for that. Now what you need to do for next week is practise the piece using method numbers 17, 22 and 90 (or whatever) from the list. Goodbye, practise well and see you next week!' Of course, there is a little more to pedagogy than that, but the idea of trying to quantify specific approaches to practising has remained, and even though it is clearly vital constantly to adopt and change one's approach to learning and refining at the keyboard, it is clearly fascinating to try to list different tactics for exploration. 'The practice list' was eventually published as two separate articles in *International Piano*, and readers are welcome to study it as it currently exists in the 'Writings' section on my website, www.murraymclachlan.co.uk. Naturally, it should always be viewed as work in progress …

The practice list can coexist happily with the standard textbooks on practising mentioned earlier in this chapter (see p.161 footnote), though it has to be pointed out that many of the possibilities the list details should be worked at simultaneously, and that the various permutations of practice points are therefore limitless. I am sure that there are many obvious and not-so-obvious methods that have been missed out, and I invite all readers freely to contribute ideas to the catalogue. Though space has limited the current number on the website to little more than 100 approaches, it should be easy to multiply that number five times over. The category approach is significant in that prior to practice you can decide which category is best suited to your current need, mood or inclination. If you are feeling impatient and excitable, for instance, then it is far better to opt for approaches from Section 2 ('Energised and rhythmic practice') than from Section 9 (concerned with work in your head rather than physically at the piano). Above all, this list should never be regarded as dogmatic – flexibility and adaptability are the bywords, and if after a few moments the list is entirely forgotten as inspiration and intuition take over in a session of pure productive joy at the piano, then no one should feel anything other than delight!

18 Memory

Why play from memory? It is only in comparatively recent times that memorising has been expected from pianists. Prior to Liszt, performers tended not to play without the music, whereas today audiences and examiners require performances without the dots in solo repertoire and concertos. There is no doubt that playing from memory can lead to a closer connection with the music and a feeling of being more at one with the instrument. Teachers often imply that printed pages act as a barrier between players and the magical, quasi-improvisatory creativity in concerts that we all strive for and which, hopefully, leads to moments of spontaneous genius. The implication is that performing with the music desk up, a hired page-turner at your side and your eyes fixed on the notes makes for stiff, awkward and earth-bound music-making.

But equally common is the scenario where memory can destroy careers. The stress and effort to achieve infallible memory can be overwhelming. It always seems such a tragic waste when you hear of students, and even professional players, who actually go so far as to terminate their careers solely because of a fear of memory lapses. I would argue that memorising for performance is extremely beneficial for those who are confident and experienced enough to cope with it, but that negative factors (stress, anxiety, breakdown in mid flow) far outweigh the possible advantages of attempted memory for players who find it all unsettling, unreliable or even terrifying. It should also be mentioned that there are today many well-known and successful artists who are able to reach transcendental heights of sublime artistry at the keyboard with a sympathetically discreet page-turner at their side. It is clearly necessary to develop the skill of being able to read music without allowing it to interfere with your freedom at the instrument, as well as to develop your listening skills as you play and your connection with the audience. I would argue that a considerable amount of practice is necessary in order to build up these necessary qualities if you choose to use music in concerts – but it will be time well spent.

Having said that, it is still important for all pianists to work on their memory skills, even if they have no intention of ever memorising in concerts. Being able to internalise the music you play makes you closer to the music. By this I mean, for example, hearing a Beethoven sonata from beginning to end in your head, with no lapses in concentration. By doing this, you will not only have a fantastic sense of security when you play – you will also be able to focus away from the piano on exactly how you wish each phrase in your music to be shaped. When viewed as a technical tool towards greater musical awareness and creativity, memory can be seen on the same level as aural awareness, improvisatory facility, compositional skills, singing and sight-reading ability. Clearly, pianists will find that their playing improves if they build up their technique and understanding in each of these areas – even though they may not necessarily wish to have their compositions or singing flagged-up for public consumption!

Practising memory techniques

So how do you 'practise' memory? How do you gain facility and ease? It is worth remembering that there are five types of memory (aural, visual, kinaesthetic, analytical and rote) and that inevitably people tend to be strong in some of these and less strong in others. **Aural memory** can be practised by playing a passage and then 'listening back' in your head. **Visual memory** is, of course, similar to memory work in other areas outside music, and is again best tackled by those without experience via small passages first. **Analytical memory** is best built up by observing the compositional techniques on the score and noting sequences, chord patterns, intervals, and so on. **Kinaesthetic memory** (really 'finger' memory) can be worked at away from the instrument, and consists of feeling the patterns, becoming familiar with them and gaining the sort of security that means you can play Beethoven's 'Appassionata' on a table top! **Rote memory** is the most boring, consisting of mechanically repeating sections over and over again in the hope that eventually they will become lodged in your head. Sadly, students tend to practise memory by rote to the exclusion of the other four aspects, and this can lead to disillusionment with the music they are preparing.

Before going any further it is worth mentioning that many musicians find that memory often develops by default: as you get deeper into the study of a piece – as you continue to listen to and refine sounds, phrasing, balancing, and so on – gradually you stop looking at the score. This can readily be seen at music festivals with very young children, who often perform their tiny pieces with the music up on the stand but never look at it!

Remember at all times that the goal in memory work is to internalise the music so that it is completely secure in your inner ear. It often takes a considerable amount of time and effort to achieve this, but it is worth the struggle – even if you never intend to perform from memory in public!

The five types of memory

In order to arrive at a more systematic and reliable methodology, it is worth separating and studying memory in the five categories listed above. Will working on each area lead to the ultimate memory goal – completely secure internalisation? Clearly, this ability needs to be developed over a considerable period of time. In order to do this, each memory category needs to be examined and practised systematically and regularly. Let's look at each in turn.

Aural memory

This is the most important for internalisation. Being able to mentally 'hear' music in your head is clearly a crucial skill. Try developing your aural memory skills by scheduling ten minutes a day for learning small segments of a piece in slow tempo. On day one the segments could be half a bar, on day two a whole bar, day three two bars, and so on. Play each section, then close your eyes and try to hear in your head exactly what you have just played. With polyphonic music, the ability to hear each part, then sing it aloud from memory away from your instrument and printed score, will do wonders. For singers and instrumentalists, too, it is useful to hear internally at least part of your accompaniment part.

Visual memory

Remembering a piece of music from the way it looks on the page is a wonderful way of learning music that is rich in textual detail. It is worth trying to extend your capabilities by allowing as much time as is necessary for your eyes to take in a section of music, no matter how small, and then close them and try to 'see' in front of you a print of the copy in your mind's eye. As with all memory work, it is crucial that you remain patient and think gradually.

Analytical memory

This involves examining the harmonies, scale patterns, phrase structures, motifs, intervals and contrapuntal devices in a passage that needs to be memorised. At its most basic level it involves stripping away all inessential notes, leaving only the basic shape or 'skeleton' of the music. It is useful to practise playing the skeleton of your music on its own, so that an awareness of the music's harmonic structure is explicitly felt. This can easily be illustrated in the C major Prelude of Bach's *The Well-Tempered Clavier*, Book 1, if each bar is compressed into chordal units in practice.

Kinaesthetic memory

Also referred to as 'finger' or 'tactile' memory, this approach involves remembering the patterns in which our fingers move over our instruments. It can be developed in a similar way to aural memory: play a small segment, then close your music and try to repeat the segment by playing the finger pattern on a work surface, or even on your knee.

Rote memory

This is the most tiring and also the least stimulating memory technique. But it can be a tolerable method of work if it is viewed from the perspective of 'working out' at the gym. Treadmill work at the keyboard may sound unmusical, but it is relatively exciting if you get a surge of adrenalin from repeating a passage over and over again, gradually looking less and less at your music, especially if you can sense success as a direct result of all the hard work.

Memory work should be cultivated and developed as an essential technical skill in the development of all performing musicians. It is not an additional asset that is tagged on after all the hard work has been done on interpretation and mechanical security. On the other hand, it is important not to become obsessive about it. Memory angst nearly always occurs when insufficient time has been scheduled for preparation, and in this sense it is no different from any other aspect of technique.

Scheduling and attitude

In order to prevent memory work from detracting from creativity and enjoyment of playing, I recommend that it is ignored in most of your practising. When you are at the piano, refine your playing. Do not waste time by worrying about remembering the dots on the printed page. The best time of day to work on memory varies from individual to individual, but I personally prefer to do it immediately before retiring for the night. Whatever time of day you choose, it is important to be relaxed and calm when you work. The biggest enemy of success in this field can be impatience, and it is all too easy to rush and do things by approximation. Utilise the micro-practising technique suggested in Chapter 17 (p.161–4). Much better to gradually refine and control small sections than to go for a broad brushstroke over several pages that will lead to hundreds of small errors. Experience has shown that if you memorise a misreading, it becomes extremely hard to get rid of it afterwards! It is therefore more sensible to work with concentration at a quiet dynamic level and a slow tempo, and to tackle memory from each of the perspectives listed above.

Advanced memory techniques

There are times when even the most talented of performers can find certain passages or pieces extremely difficult to memorise, even when they religiously follow guidelines from teachers and standard textbooks. Nowadays, when examination requirements at conservatoire level often insist on students memorising all presented repertoire up to 1945, teachers are faced with the challenge of how to help students as they struggle to overcome seemingly impossible tests to their memory.

From a psychological standpoint, having a memory lapse in even the smallest section of a work can have a hugely negative effect on a pianist's interpretation of the entire piece. Being preoccupied with issues of memory whilst performing can result in a pianist concentrating too much on reaching the end of a piece rather than enjoying playing the piece itself (so-called 'end-gaining'), and this in turn can lead to a lack of attention towards phrasing, rhythmic stability, details, pedalling and all other aspects of interpretation. More seriously, memory blocks can result in physical tension, a lack of self-esteem and a lowering of enthusiasm for piano playing in general. So what can be done? The following 'emergency rescue tips' for memory have proved very effective in practice, provided the pianist has sufficient patience and determination.

Let's look at three challenging fragments in examples from different periods of the repertoire: the first movement of Bach's A minor English Suite; the central section of Chopin's E flat minor Étude, Op.10 No.6; and the transition from chorale to fugue in César Franck's Prelude, Chorale and Fugue.

J.S. Bach: English Suite in A minor, first movement, bars 47–50

Chopin: Étude in E flat minor, Op.10 No.6, bars 29–32

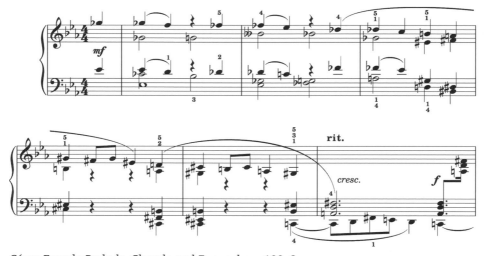

César Franck: Prelude, Chorale and Fugue, bars 122–8

Begin by memorising miniscule sections, and then build up the length of the sections as your familiarity with the music increases. Go through this list strictly in turn:

1 **Lie down on the floor and relax.** Take deep breaths and banish negative thoughts. Live in the present – stop thinking ahead. Instead of thinking 'what if I cannot memorise this?' simply look forward to playing and experiencing beautiful music. When you have achieved this, go to the piano.

2 **Posture and breathing.** Sitting at the piano, relax and take deep breaths (do this regularly throughout your work on improving your memory). To help you to relax, walk around the room every five minutes.

3 **Simultaneously sing and play the main melodic thread in the passage.** Repeat this several times, alternating between reading the music and playing from memory with your eyes closed. This melodic thread is your 'lifeline': even if you forget all the other notes in the passage, if you continue to play the main melodic thread you will avoid stopping. In the excerpt shown above, the beautiful complexities of Franck's writing mean that the four melodic strands are equally important, and they should be practised, sung and played individually, with each line repeated three or four times at each practice session until secure.

4 **Play the main cadences and chord progressions in the passage** (it may be helpful to play these in pairs). Emphasise the top, middle and bottom notes in each chord with each repetition, and try singing the notes as you play them. Alternate between reading the music and playing the chords in pairs from memory with your eyes shut. In the examples from Bach, Chopin and Franck above, the chord progressions are marked clearly so that in practice it will be easy to 'extract' them from the passages in order to gain security in memory via repetitive practice with variations in voicing.

5 **Study the music away from the piano,** noting the main chords, keys, intervals, dynamics and articulation.

6 **Think of the character, the colours, and the physical approach** required for each bar.

7 **At the piano, keep your eyes on the music** and play through the piece at a dynamic of ***ppp*** and with no pedal.

8 **Keeping your eyes on the music, play the left-hand part aloud but the right-hand part silently** (by just slightly depressing the keys). Repeat by playing the right-hand part aloud, and the left-hand part silently.

9 **Away from the piano, write out the fingering of each note** then play (using the music) the passage on a table following the exact fingering.

10 **Copy fingering onto a piece of paper and play the piece on a table or work surface.** Repeat this exercise with your eyes shut. Alternate between looking at the paper with the fingerings, and closing your eyes.

11 **Copy the music note-for-note onto manuscript paper**, firstly from the printed text, secondly from memory. As you do this, ensure that you can 'hear' and 'play' the notes silently.

12 **Play the passage on your knees.** Perhaps surprisingly, this is fun to do. By taking away the sonic element from the note patterns completely, it quickly strengthens finger (kinaesthetic) memory.

13 **Away from the piano, 'play' the complete passage in your head.** If it helps to move your fingers as you do this, then fine, but ideally you should be able to simply hear the section in your head.

14 **Lie down and 'sing' the passage in your head and aloud.** If you can sing the left hand alone from memory, then the right hand alone, then 'play' it in your head hands together, the passage will be extremely secure.

15 **Play the passage and record yourself; listen to the recording and note any areas that went wrong.** If necessary, repeat the entire process for that particular place again until the problem ceases.

If you can remain calm and live in the present whilst working through this list of fifteen tasks for more than a few days of practising, then you will find success. Though it is obviously vital for students to tackle memory issues with intelligence and systematic endeavour on a daily basis, it is fair to say that stress and impatience are the most common reasons for failure in this area. But that is not a reason to give up: even if you finally choose not to play a particularly challenging work with the music propped up on the stand during a performance, working at memorisation via the concentrated practice techniques listed above will certainly improve your technical security and musical awareness – provided you remain calm and philosophical!

Tips for improving memory

- Separate work on memorising your repertoire from practising your repertoire.

- Find the best time of day for you as an individual to work on memory. This is often different from the time of day that you feel happiest practising (many find last thing at night the most effective place to schedule in memory work).

- De-stress! It is extremely difficult to work on memory if you are tense, anxious or impatient. Begin your memory sessions with some relaxation techniques and meditation.

- Work in bite-size segments that are well within your capabilities. Never try to cut corners or jump ahead by aiming immediately for memory of large sections.

- Attack memory on all five fronts: aurally, visually, analytically, kinaesthetically and by rote.

- Internalise! Total confidence and security will emerge in memory when you can play through your entire repertoire inside your head, away from your music and instrument, whilst walking down the street. This is the ideal aim for anyone who really wishes to be secure in his or her preparation for a concert performance.

- Sleep, eat, drink and exercise like an athlete.

- Be philosophical: realise that memory takes time, is mysterious and will often defy orders! It is often when you least expect success, and have nearly given up all hope of ever being able to memorise a passage, that security and fluency will emerge.